D0265207

DAMIEN
DUFF

DAMIEN DUFF

THE BIOGRAPHY

JOEL MILLER

JOHN BLAKE

John Blake Publishing
Published by John Blake Publishing Ltd,
3 Bramber Court, 2 Bramber Road,
London W14 9PB, UK
www.blake.co.uk

First published in hardback in 2007

ISBN: 978-1-84454-331-1

All rights reserved. No part of this publication may be reproduced, stored in a
retrieval system, or in any form or by any means, without the prior permission
in writing of the publisher, nor be otherwise circulated in any form of binding
or cover other than that in which it is published and without a similar
condition including this condition being imposed on the subsequent publisher.

British Library Cataloguing-in-Publication Data:
A catalogue record for this book is available from the British Library.

Design by www.envydesign.co.uk

Printed and bound in Great Britain by William Clowes Ltd, Beccles, Suffolk

1 3 5 7 9 10 8 6 4 2

Text copyright © Joel Miller, 2007

Photographs courtesy of Clevamedia, Getty Images, Rex Features,
Action Images and Empics.

Papers used by John Blake Publishing are natural, recyclable products made
from wood grown in sustainable forests. The manufacturing processes
conform to the environmental regulations of the country of origin.

Every effort has been made to contact relevant copyright holders.
Any omission is inadvertent; we would be grateful if the appropriate
people could contact us.

Contents

Prologue vii

CHAPTER 1: Ballyboden Boy 1

CHAPTER 2: Park Life 11

CHAPTER 3: Dreams of Green 23

CHAPTER 4: Growing Pains 39

CHAPTER 5: Far Eastern Promise 61

CHAPTER 6: Survival Instincts 95

CHAPTER 7: Domestic Bliss 117

CHAPTER 8: Great Expectations 133

CHAPTER 9: And It's Goodbye From Him... 147

CHAPTER 10: World Cup Wonders 161

CHAPTER 11: A Wanted Man 183

CHAPTER 12: Blue is the Colour 207

CHAPTER 13: Special Delivery   237

CHAPTER 14: Frustrating Finale   255

CHAPTER 15: New Kid in Toon   271

Prologue

For fans of Newcastle United the summer of 2006 was an uncertain time. Fresh from bidding an emotional farewell to the revered Alan Shearer, they were faced with the prospect of life without a player whose legendary status at St James' Park had long been assured by the time he claimed his 206th and final goal for the club.

It was the end of an era, and after serving his hometown team with great distinction for ten years Newcastle's record goalscorer had pulled on the famous black and white number-nine shirt for the last time.

As a result, his adoring following needed a new hero to worship. One man capable of filling the void left by Shearer's retirement was another free-scoring England centre-forward, Michael Owen. The former Liverpool striker had made a decent start to his Newcastle career after joining from Real

Madrid, and despite missing half the previous season after breaking a bone in his foot, his notable presence was expected to inspire Glenn Roeder's men in the forthcoming campaign.

That was until he sustained a serious knee injury when twisting awkwardly during the opening moments of England's World Cup encounter with Sweden in Cologne. Owen was set for a long spell on the sidelines and Roeder was forced to look elsewhere for a new talisman. He needed someone to inject some fresh hope into the club, a crowd-pleaser capable of giving the whole place a much-needed lift.

His search saw him land a player who fitted the bill perfectly. A two-time Premiership champion with more than fifty international caps to his name and, at twenty-seven years of age, about to reach his prime. Damien Duff was just the man for the job.

A senior international since the age of nineteen and one of the game's most exciting and versatile wingers, Duff had delighted followers of Blackburn Rovers, Chelsea and the Republic of Ireland with a devastating combination of pace and trickery. Now it was the turn of Newcastle's Toon Army to savour his skills, just as they'd marvelled in the past at other masters of the dribble, Chris Waddle, Paul Gascoigne and David Ginola.

At various stages of his career, Duff had even been compared to the greatest dribbler of them all, George Best, by a number of esteemed figures within the game. In fact, lofty comparisons and gushing praise were both regular features of his career.

'I have played with some brilliant players during my career, but I've never seen a talent like Damien Duff,' former

Prologue

Blackburn teammate Craig Hignett once told the *Observer*. 'Gazza was special and Juninho was a little box of tricks, but neither had the explosive skills that Damien possesses.'

A man so well renowned for his love of sleep that the term 'adhesive-mattress syndrome' was coined especially for him, Duff displayed an easygoing demeanour off the pitch that had always stood in great contrast to his explosive nature on it.

'He sleeps for almost every second that he's not playing football,' revealed Niall Quinn in his autobiography. In the same book, the former Ireland striker paid a more considered tribute to a player he'd seen develop from overawed teenager to World Cup star right in front of his eyes. 'The game has hardly touched Damien Duff,' Quinn wrote. 'He's not hard. He has no ego.'

What Duff did have in July 2006 was a new employer and with it a new challenge, namely to arouse a club that had failed to win a major domestic trophy since 1955, despite several false dawns and near misses.

Duff had become used to playing a part in bringing long, unproductive spells to an end. At Blackburn he helped the club win a major cup for the first time in seventy-four years, and his maiden title success at Stamford Bridge ended Chelsea's fifty-year wait for the championship.

Newcastle fans were hoping he had one more revival job left in him.

CHAPTER 1

Ballyboden Boy

'Dribbling the ball? I don't know where it came from.
I always liked it. It was always my thing.'

DAMIEN DUFF, MAY 2002

ONE March night in 1979, in the swanky surroundings of the London Hilton Hotel, Arsenal's Liam Brady received the most prestigious of English football's individual awards when he was named Player of the Year by the Professional Footballers' Association. It was the ultimate nod of recognition from his contemporaries, and underlined the brilliant Dublin-born midfielder's status as the most creative player ever to have emerged from the southern half of the Emerald Isle. Little did he know it, but roughly 300 miles away on the other side of the Irish Sea, a future contender for his crown was stirring.

Damien Anthony Duff was born on 2 March 1979. The third of Gerry and Mary Duff's five children, he grew up in the sedate surroundings of Ballyboden on the south side of Dublin's River Liffey, barely five miles from the famous old

Lansdowne Road ground around which young Damien's name would one day reverberate.

It was 'a typical, close-knit Irish family', according to the middle child, but the head of the household's leading interest had a huge influence on the spare-time activities of his offspring. Gerry Duff's love of football meant that his boys would inevitably follow suit.

'Dad is soccer-mad and he threw a football at me almost as soon as I could walk,' Duff once told the *Irish Times*. It was a wise move from his father, and one for which supporters of Blackburn Rovers, Chelsea and Newcastle United – not to mention those of the national team – would at various stages in the future be extremely grateful.

Having been presented with a ball by his 'Da' at such a tender age, the toddler who would mature into Ireland's most expensive player of all time was rarely seen without one in the years that followed. There was a brief flirtation with rugby, but that came and went. Damien Duff's dreams were fired by football.

The sparkling array of skills that have dazzled some of the best defenders in the world were honed on the streets, fields and playgrounds of his home patch. The deft twists and turns, the immaculate close control, the graceful poise and a devastating attacking instinct – the mastering of each resulted from endless hours of endeavour and a boundless enthusiasm for the sport.

'If he wasn't playing in a game or training, chances were he would be found outside knocking the ball off the wall,' said his mother Mary, in the *News of the World*. 'There is a crack in the wall now and I believe it is from the amount of times he used to hit the ball against it.'

It wasn't that Duff felt a necessity to practise: he just *wanted* to play football. All the time. He loved having a ball at his feet, and has retained that youthful zest for the game throughout his professional career. At his most brilliant, he performs in the same free-spirited manner as one imagines he exhibited while tearing about the park as a young boy.

That devotion to football was intensified in his formative years by the achievements of Jack Charlton and his historic Republic of Ireland side. Duff belonged to a starry-eyed generation of Irish youngsters who watched in awe as their country made its presence felt on the grandest of stages. If you were growing up in Dublin at the back end of the 1980s, then footballing heroes were certainly not in short supply.

Not that there'd been a dearth of Irish stars before that. Noel Cantwell, Charlie Hurley, Johnny Giles, Liam Brady and Frank Stapleton were all rightfully idolised in their respective eras. The trouble was, they never had the opportunity to display their talents at a gathering of the game's elite.

Under Big Jack, though, things would change. First, in 1988, his team beat England 1–0 in their opening game of the European Championships. Every player in emerald green was afforded legendary status in an instant, and even though a 1–1 draw with the Soviet Union and an agonising 1–0 defeat against Holland cut short Ireland's first ever appearance at the European finals, the Irish public – including a nine-year-old Damien Duff – had been captivated by the whole experience.

Two years later, Charlton's boys ensured another

unforgettable summer for the watching millions back home when Ireland appeared at the World Cup finals for the first time. Defeat to hosts Italy resulted in a quarter-final exit, but only after comeback draws against England and Holland and a thrilling penalty shootout victory over Romania had seen the debutants leave an indelible mark on the competition.

If any doubts about his future ambitions had been lingering in the mind of the young Duff, then the national team's heroics erased them in conclusive fashion. He wanted to be a footballer, and he knew exactly whose boots he wanted to fill.

Not those of Ray Houghton, the match winner against England in Stuttgart, or those of World Cup penalty shootout heroes Packie Bonner or David O'Leary. Not even Big Paul McGrath, a rock at the heart of Ireland's defence, could claim to be Duff's favourite player.

That title belonged to a midfielder whose wand of a left foot helped Everton dominate the English game in the mid-eighties and – more pertinently – rifled home an equaliser for Ireland against England in their 1990 World Cup encounter in Cagliari.

'It was all to do with Kevin Sheedy's left foot,' Duff has since told the *Sunday Mirror*. 'We watched every minute of football on TV that we could get our hands on. I remember watching those European Championships in Germany and then every second of the World Cup two years later. I was a big Ireland fan back then and, if you were a left-footer, Kevin Sheedy was the player to be. Every time we played football out on the street or in the schoolyard, I wanted to be Kevin Sheedy.'

Celtic and Manchester United were the clubs he longed to play for, but the first shirt in which Duff paraded his skills was that of Leicester Celtic, a local outfit based in Rathfarnham. He joined them at the age of eight and naturally took to the wing because, even back then, he'd already developed a tendency to take players on.

'Dribbling the ball? I don't know where it came from,' Duff said in an interview with the *Irish Times* some years later. 'I always liked it. I'd do it on my own when I was a kid. I don't know. It was always my thing. I don't like to overdo it, though, the dribbling. I hope it doesn't look like it. I've always had good coaches, but they just let me get on with it. If I try it on too much they're the first to tell me.'

It wasn't long before the boy from Ballyboden was demonstrating the sort of artistry and attacking flair that would eventually take him to the top of the game.

Leicester Celtic chairman Brian Delaney for one is unlikely to forget the impact made by the spindly little blond kid who was shy and reserved away from the pitch but explosive from the moment he stepped onto it.

'Damien started playing for us at under-nine level and the manager, Paddy Cosgrove, assured me this young fellow would go all the way,' Delaney told the *News of the World*. 'He had natural ability – you didn't have to teach him anything. Damien would drop his shoulder and just go past players. He didn't want to pass to anyone, such was his confidence. From early morning until nightfall he would be practising with the ball.'

The young Duff soon acquired something of a reputation,

and opponents knew exactly where Leicester's main threat was coming from. One such opponent was Alan Maybury, who was playing for Home Farm in an under-11s cup final when he first came face to face with the trickster whom everyone was talking about.

'[Duff] was playing for Leicester Celtic then,' recalls Maybury, who would later make his senior international debut on the same night as his former foe. 'I can remember us being warned about "that tricky little left winger – we have to watch that fella". He stood out then. I used to play centre-back, so I never marked him, thankfully – I'd rather play with him than against him, that's for sure.'

Those involved at youth level in Dublin weren't the only ones sitting up and taking notice. Whispers of Duff's emergence as one of the area's brightest young things were starting to spread further afield.

Former Ireland international Ray Treacy, who was capped forty-two times in the 1960s and 1970s, was initially sceptical when he heard the rumours, but soon changed his tack. Talking to the *Sunday Mirror* in 2003, he said, 'Everyone knew about him. It happens like that in Dublin. It may be a big city but the grapevine is very small and we all heard about this kid called Duff out with Leicester. You hear talk like that all the time. There are about ten Liam Bradys born every year in Dublin if you listen to the hype but this one was true. Duffer is as good now as it was claimed he was going to be then – and there are few Irish players you can say that about.'

The wispy winger's form had generated a great deal of

interest around the capital, but, just as he seemed set for the next stage of his development, Duff promptly turned his back on the game.

In a surprising switch he discovered a new form of activity when he went to a secondary school – De La Salle College in Churchtown, Dublin – where the preferred sport was played with an oval ball. Rugby was now the game of choice for Duff, and, having spent the early years of his sporting life terrorising opposing full-backs, he suddenly found himself occupying precisely that position – albeit in a very different discipline.

In an interview with the *News of the World* published during Duff's first full season as a Blackburn player, his mother Mary explained how her son's life could easily have taken an alternative path.

'Football was Damien's favourite but he got into rugby when he started attending De La Salle College in Churchtown,' she said. 'He was good at it because he was always in the college team playing at full-back. He took it so seriously, in fact, he played little or no football for about two years to focus more on his rugby. Then he started to get back into soccer but I became worried he would end up drained from playing so much.

'For his own good I told him he would have to give up one of them. He decided to stick with football and he hasn't looked back. Sometimes I wonder how he might have got on had he opted to continue playing rugby. Who knows, maybe he would be a budding Irish player now but I think he made the right choice.'

Duff's sporting swap was the source of some frustration for

those who had been keeping a close eye on his progress, none more so than Tony McNally of Lourdes Celtic. He tried his best to lure Duff to the Dublin club but, as he revealed to the *Mirror*, his initial approach was rebuffed.

'When I saw him he was the greatest player I'd seen,' McNally said of Duff. 'He was a born player. He did not really need coaching. There were others who were more street-wise, but no one had the same talent.

'We thought we'd lost him for good when he went to De La Salle, which only plays rugby. However, I think his dad wanted him to play with Lourdes because he played with them himself. You never know, if Damien had not changed his mind he could now be playing rugby with Brian O'Driscoll in the Irish team.'

He did change his mind, though, and McNally's persistence finally paid off when Duff agreed to become a Lourdes Celtic player. For a lad who later reflected that 'soccer was my first love', his return to the game was almost inevitable.

Picking up from where he'd left off was not a problem. The destructive nature of his feet had not been numbed by his period of inactivity, and Damien Duff the footballer was once again hot property. At that stage, though, his frail-looking frame deterred any potential suitors, according to McNally.

'We eventually got him to come over to the club but he was so shy he would just sit on the stool with his head down and would say nothing,' he added. 'But when he went out on the field he was completely different and eventually he came out of his shell.

'Damien was very small and everyone thought he wasn't

tough enough to mix it in the Premiership. I had confidence he could make it but my confidence wasn't shared by scouts from the big British clubs. They came to look at him but they weren't impressed with what they saw. They kept saying he was too small and that he couldn't cut it in England. But I told them they would regret it.'

Ed Roach, the secretary of Lourdes Celtic, did share McNally's confidence in the promising youngster. 'Damien was milky white and looked like he would blow away in a strong gust, but he was hard as steel,' he said. 'He was quiet as a mouse and he listened to everything and learned all he could. And he had so much belief in his ability that he would try things with the ball no other kid would dare.'

Liverpool were among those British clubs not entirely convinced of Duff's credentials. 'I told Liverpool about Damien when he was a schoolboy at Lourdes Celtic,' Irish scout Noel McCabe explained to the *Express* in 2003.

'At the time he would have swum across the Irish Sea to sign for an English club and Liverpool were ahead of the posse. They did watch him in a schoolboy international, but the following week I got a call and was told they didn't think he had much between the ears because he kept getting caught offside. It was a real kick in the teeth for me because I knew how good Damien was.'

Teachers at De La Salle remember Duff as a quiet, easygoing student who was bright and diligent and dedicated to his schoolwork. In the long run, though, the academic life was not for him, and he made that perfectly clear when filling out a careers form at school during his early teenage years.

He'd enjoyed his brush with rugby but his love for the game that first captured his imagination remained undiminished. His desired profession? Footballer.

'It was the big joke at the time,' Duff revealed to the *Irish Times* almost a decade later. 'I put it down on a form. Footballer. They'd never had that before. The teacher had a word with my Ma. I think she had to explain that it was serious. What could they say? If I hadn't the football I'd probably be bumming around sitting in a bar every night.'

CHAPTER 2
Park Life

'Once Damien met Kenny his mind was made up.'
GERRY DUFF, JUNE 2002

'Damien was special,' recalls Pat Devlin, casting his mind back to a day that would ultimately change the fortunes of both himself and the boy he stood marvelling at. 'That first time I saw him play, I knew he was the one. I've often compared spotting him to walking into a nightclub and seeing the girl of your dreams. Well, it was a bit like that for me, the first time I saw Damien play. He was 13 and I hung my hat on him.'

Pat Devlin, speaking on that occasion to the *Mirror*, is a well-known character in Irish football. Not for his achievements as a player – he appeared once for the Ireland youth team – but for the various roles in which he has operated since calling a halt to his playing days.

The bulk of his time as a manager has been spent with Eircom League club Bray Wanderers, while he's also enjoyed spells with Shamrock Rovers, Athlone Town and Drogheda United. In April 2006 Steve Staunton brought him into the international fold, placing him in charge of the B team and appointing him Eircom League coordinator in a bid to develop home-based players.

Devlin has also worked as a scout for a string of English clubs. In the mid-1980s, soon after he was first handed the managerial reins at Bray, Liverpool asked him to keep an eye out for emerging talent in Ireland. It was from there that he formed a lasting association with Kenny Dalglish.

By the early nineties, Dalglish had moved on to Blackburn Rovers, and Devlin had switched his allegiance accordingly. His brief was the same: find the future stars of Ireland. Soon enough, he came across one.

'He flicked the ball over the centre-half, repeated this when the full-back came at him and then slipped it past the keeper,' he said, recalling another early glimpse of the Duff magic. 'You just cannot coach that into someone – that's natural ability and it was the moment when I said to myself, "Yeah, he'll do for me."

'Other sides would put their biggest guy on Duffer with instructions to kick him out of the game,' he told the *News of the World*. 'Well, they simply couldn't get near him. He was too fast for them physically and mentally and that speed of thought is still the key to his success today. He is two or three moves ahead of whoever happens to be marking him. He knows what he is going to do long before the defender realises it.

'Damien was a shy lad. You would hardly get a word out

of him but when he did talk it was almost always about football. And he didn't just talk, he listened to what was said to him about his game and always took it on board.'

Duff was enticed away from Lourdes Celtic by another club, St Kevin's, where he further enhanced his burgeoning reputation. 'Damien was a very, very quiet, nice, well-mannered lad,' remembered coach Ken O'Donoghue in the *Independent on Sunday*. 'You knew immediately, though, that he was special.'

Another, more glamorous, move was on the horizon for Duff. Several clubs from England were expressing an interest, and Pat Devlin knew that he had some work to do if Blackburn were to get their man.

So he arranged a friendly between the Ireland Under-15s and a Blackburn team from the same age group. Duff was in the Ireland team, as was future Westlife star Nicky Byrne, and Kenny Dalglish was among those in attendance. Ireland won 3–0, Duff scored and Dalglish was suitably impressed.

'Duffer stole the show and Kenny decided on the spot to take him on,' reckons Devlin.

So far, so good, then. Devlin, however, still had one concern. Duff's mother and father were brought over to view the area that their son would soon be calling home, but Devlin wasn't convinced that taking them to the site of Blackburn's new Brockhall training complex was a wise move.

'I thought Blackburn were going to blow it,' Devlin told the *Sunday Express*. 'There wasn't too much to see because most of the complex was still at the planning stage. All you could see were loads of cows. But Mary and Gerry said it was ideal for their son – nice and peaceful.'

The clinching factor was the identity of the man in charge at Rovers. Kenny Dalglish's standing in the game was immense, and the young Duff couldn't help but be impressed by the Liverpool legend.

'I thought Kenny was funny and I thought overall it was the place to be,' he later told the *Irish Times*. 'I was just dying to go.

'I wasn't the first to go over. Alan Maybury, Nicky Byrne out of Westlife and Damien Lynch all went to Leeds at the same time. There was a good few went before me, but you're that age and you want to go away and see what it's like. Pat Devlin was pals with Dalglish at Blackburn and Pat put a lot of pressure on me to go to Blackburn... a lot of persuasion there from Pat. Thanks be to God I took the hint anyway.'

So that, pretty much, was that. All parties came to an agreement and Damien Duff became a Blackburn Rovers player. Pat Devlin had played a key part in the move, and the Duffs clearly saw him as someone they could trust. So much so that Devlin became his young protégé's adviser, and would remain close to Duff and his family throughout the years.

Damien Duff's career path would have been very different had he taken his father's advice. Gerry Duff was concerned, first of all, that things were happening too quickly for his son and he felt he would be better off staying at school and completing his education.

Secondly, Duff Sr was worried that moving to a

Premiership outfit such as Blackburn, where competition for places would be fierce, could hamper young Damien's chances of making it. He wasn't entirely sure that Ewood Park was the most suitable destination and, if he'd had his way, his boy would have been running out in the blue and white of Huddersfield Town.

'We had a constant stream of scouts knocking on the door trying to get Damien to sign for them,' Gerry has since told the *Mirror*.

'Clubs had come in with offers of trials and, strange as it seems, I was keen on him going to Huddersfield. I liked what I saw at the club and their manager Neil Warnock impressed me when I spoke to him. I also probably felt there was a better chance of Damien getting into the first team there.

'But meeting Kenny was the big thing for Damien. I had been very impressed by Huddersfield, but once Damien met Kenny his mind was made up.

'I wanted him to stay and finish off at school but Damien's mind was made up. This, he told me, was a "once-in-a-lifetime opportunity". So I said fine, and told him we'd always be there for him if things didn't work out. And then he said to me – "I won't be back". Now Damien is far from big-headed but even then he had enough self-confidence to believe he could make a living out of the game.'

Nineteen ninety-five was a good year for Blackburn Rovers. Not only did the club become top-flight champions for the first time in eighty-one years, but a sixteen-year-old kid named Damien Duff became a permanent member of the playing staff. For a young boy who'd grown up in such a close family unit, leaving home presented Duff with a huge challenge, although the excitement generated by the prospect of representing the newly crowned kings of England helped overcome any initial difficulties.

For Mary Duff, seeing one of her fledglings fly the nest was particularly hard. Because Damien was under the age of eighteen, his parents had to sign a consent form before he could join Blackburn, placing Mrs Duff in something of a quandary. Some years later, when she was invited onto Marian Finucane's radio show in the wake of her son's 2002 World Cup heroics, Mary revealed the anguish she'd faced in letting him go.

'I didn't think Damien would go away, though I knew that was what he wanted,' she said. 'But I thought he wouldn't go because he's a real home bird. The parents have to sign because he was under eighteen, to say we were allowing him to go. I didn't want him to sign and he said he'd never forgive me if I didn't let him go. Looking back, I'm delighted I did sign.'

The opportunity of joining a leading Premiership club had been too good to turn down for Duff. All he'd ever wanted to do was play football and now that was exactly what he was doing. Every day. It was the life he'd been dreaming of long before he'd inserted the word *footballer* in the 'Desired Profession?' box on his school careers form.

What he hadn't considered, though, was the prospect of homesickness. His dreams had seen him running defenders ragged and scoring spectacular goals, not sitting around feeling lonely in unfamiliar surroundings. Once the honeymoon period had elapsed and the initial excitement had worn off, Duff began yearning for his cherished home life. Adjusting to his new existence was proving harder than he'd imagined.

His second year was particularly difficult, and things came to a head when Duff approached Ray Harford, the man who'd succeeded Kenny Dalglish as first-team manager at Blackburn, to tell him he'd had enough. He wanted to go home.

'Every weekend, when the English lads would get to go home, I'd be in tears,' Duff later reflected, in the *Sunday Times*. 'Once every six weeks wasn't enough for me. I didn't care, I just wanted to go home. I went into Ray Harford's office. Standing in front of him, I broke down in tears, but Ray, God rest his soul, was great. He explained that it wouldn't be right for me to give it up.

'He said wait, hold on a minute. Calm down and all that. And by that evening they were flying the Ma and Da over. They came and stayed for a week or 10 days with me and I got my head back on track.'

It was a caring touch by the club, and from there Duff never looked back. As well as Harford there were several other influential figures around Ewood Park to whom he could always turn for advice.

One was Tim Sherwood, the captain of Blackburn's Premiership-winning side whose boots Duff cleaned as an apprentice. Another was Alan Irvine, the former Everton winger and then Rovers' youth-team coach. Not only did Irvine play an important part in developing Duff's wing-craft, he also coined a nickname that would stick throughout his career.

'When I think of the people who influenced me, my family comes first,' Duff added. 'Then there are two coaches, Alan Irvine and Brian Kerr. I think it was Alan who started calling me "Duffer"; with his Scottish accent, he used to put "er" on to most things. But I love it, I used to have it on my boots. It's me nickname, even me mam and dad have started calling me Duffer now.'

Having settled into life off the pitch, Duff continued to thrive on it. Shortly after his seventeenth birthday he signed professional forms, and it was around this time that he received a maiden call-up to the first-team squad.

In March 1996 Rovers, who were still reigning champions but not in the reckoning for a second consecutive title, travelled to Tottenham for a Premiership fixture. On the team coach for that trip were several of the seasoned pros who had fired Blackburn to glory in the previous campaign, imposing characters such as Alan Shearer, Tim Flowers, Chris Sutton, Colin Hendry and Mike Newell. Elsewhere on the bus were a couple of seventeen-year-old boys keeping a very low profile.

Duff and Damien Johnson had been two of the Blackburn youth team's star performers that term – another was future England striker James Beattie – and the pair were rewarded for their impressive form with a trip to White Hart Lane.

'I don't know if I thought I'd make it at that time,' Duff told the *Irish Times* in 2002. 'I was just working hard and you'd get those trips and think, well, even if I have to go back with my tail between my legs at least I went with the first team once or twice. It was hard. The first one was to Spurs. Me and Damien Johnson. Me and him sitting together on the coach with our heads down hoping nobody would notice us. Then we had a room together, all our meals together, sat beside each other at the match, came back. Never spoke to anyone else.'

Neither of the youngsters appeared in the match, but the experience of watching Shearer grab a hat-trick in Rovers' 3–2 win left them desperate for more.

Also on the playing staff at Ewood Park was an Irish goalkeeper called Shay Given, who had joined the club after leaving Celtic. Three years Duff's senior, Given was another player who had been coaxed to Blackburn by Pat Devlin. He remembers being blown away by his young compatriot.

'I remember him at 16 or 17 when he first joined up with us,' Given later told the *Sunday Times*. 'You could tell early on how good he was. He was different class. Even at that age he used to go down and train with some of the first team players, he had that natural ability about him. He's a special player. He can do special things and see special passes.'

A few months after that first-team encounter at Tottenham, Duff was included in the Blackburn squad for a pre-season trip to Holland. There he caught the eye when Rovers took on Vitesse Arnhem in a friendly tournament, even keeping his cool to score a penalty in a shootout defeat. Blackburn knew they had a potential star on their hands, and the secret was in danger of leaking out.

'I have never had any doubts about Damien, he's a

natural,' Ray Harford told the *Lancashire Evening Telegraph*. 'But it is important not to rush him. We don't want to do that and we won't. He wasn't far away last year, even though there was a great deal of pressure on us, and I have no doubt that he is going to be a player.'

Harford was right but, unfortunately for the man who assisted Kenny Dalglish in Rovers' title-winning campaign of 1994–5, he wouldn't be at the club to see Duff mature into a first-team regular.

At the end of October 1996, with Blackburn bottom of the Premiership, a 1–0 home defeat to Stockport County in the League Cup proved to be the final straw. Harford resigned and Tony Parkes, a long-serving member of the backroom staff at Ewood Park, was temporarily placed in charge.

Damien Duff, meanwhile, continued to shine. He helped Blackburn reach the FA Youth Cup semi-finals and on the last day of the season – by which time Parkes had safely guided Rovers to Premiership safety – he received another first-team call-up. This time, though, he wouldn't be just a passive onlooker.

'It was Friday afternoon and I was at home resting when Tony Parkes rang to tell me I was in the squad, probably as a substitute,' Duff later recalled. 'An hour before the game Tony told me I was actually going to start and that he'd kept it back to stop me getting uptight. For a split second I felt quite faint, but the nervousness soon wore off and the other lads really helped me through.'

On Sunday, 11 May 1997, Damien Duff became a

Premiership player. A glance at Rovers' starting XI for the visit of Leicester City that day – Flowers, Kenna, Hendry, Pearce, Le Saux, McKinlay, Sherwood, Flitcroft, Duff, Gallacher and Fenton – may glean what seems of little significance now, but, for the eighteen-year-old lad lining up on the left wing, it was an occasion to savour.

The outcome of the match wasn't ideal for the home side, as Leicester romped to a 4–2 victory with Emile Heskey bagging a couple of goals. But at least the 25,881 present at Ewood Park that afternoon saw plenty of action. They also got their first glimpse of a player whose magical feet would conjure up some unforgettable moments in years to come.

'Duff, only 18, made his Premiership bow and didn't disappoint with skill and a stream of crosses from the left' was the *Lancashire Evening Telegraph*'s assessment.

'I remember it like it was yesterday,' Duff has said. 'Even though we lost, I got the man-of-the-match award and I was just buzzing. I was over the moon.'

CHAPTER 3

Dreams of Green

'I will play international football until I drop.
I love it and I treasure every Irish cap I have.'
DAMIEN DUFF, FEBRUARY 2004

If there's one thing that Damien Duff loves more than playing football, it's playing football for Ireland. Wearing the emerald-green shirt of his country has always brought out the best in him, and the proud Dubliner's showing at the World Under-20s Championship of 1997 gave early evidence of that.

Fresh from making his Premiership debut on the final day of the 1996–7 campaign, Duff was bursting with confidence as he travelled to Malaysia for the summer tournament with the rest of Brian Kerr's Irish squad. Even so, his inclusion in the group hadn't been a formality. At just eighteen, he would be giving away a couple of years to most other competitors, and Kerr needed to be sure that he was ready; a closer look at the boy in action soon convinced him of that.

Speaking to the *Sunday Mirror* in 2003, Kerr said, 'I had

just started out as the manager of the Irish Under-20s team going to Malaysia and I had known about Damien's potential for quite some time. He was three years younger than most of the lads but I just had to take a chance on him. We played him in a few trial games and he was just brilliant so I had no worries throwing him in at that level.

'Another kid called Robbie Keane also played in the practice games before we went and was magic – but there was no way I could take two so young. Damien got the nod and he was the star of the tournament.'

Duff was indeed one of the tournament's outstanding players and for that his manager deserved a great deal of credit. Kerr knew exactly how to cajole match-winning performances out of his young gem, and he has since explained his approach in an interview with the *Irish Times*.

'I remember spending a lot of time telling the team about conserving energy in matches, not to be gung-ho, not to spend all their energy,' he said. 'We'd talk about tactics and patience. One day I called Damien aside and said to him: "None of this applies to you, you can do what you want, go with your hunches." And he looked at me, very suspiciously. "Why?" he asked. "Because you're nearly always right," I said. "Go with your instincts." '

Ireland lost their first game 2–1 to Ghana, but a victory by the same scoreline against the USA and a 1–1 draw with China were enough to take them into the second round.

Duff then took centre stage. Despite suffering from food poisoning before Ireland's second round meeting with Morocco, the Blackburn starlet mustered up the game's decisive strike. Six minutes into extra time he fooled a defender and beat the goalkeeper with an exquisite finish to score the first ever golden goal in a FIFA tournament and secure a 2–1 win for his team.

Next up for Ireland was Spain, and, in previewing the quarter-final tie, the *Sunday Times* paid Duff a glowing tribute:

> Ireland have in Damien Duff the kind of player capable of producing match-winning flashes of quality. The Dubliner, who turned 18 in March, has a talismanic effect on the team and shook off a bout of food poisoning to sink Morocco with a mazy goal. Recognition at senior international level is surely a question of when, rather than if.

A 1–0 win against Spain set up a semi-final clash with Argentina, the team who'd eliminated an England side that included Michael Owen, Jamie Carragher and Danny Murphy in the second round.

The Argentines boasted a fine array of talent, with future stars Pablo Aimar, Juan Roman Riquelme and Esteban Cambiasso all displaying great promise. Just as they had done against England, Argentina found a way to overcome the Irish challenge, and a 1–0 win for the eventual winners of the tournament saw off Brian Kerr's boys.

It wasn't quite the end for Ireland, though, and especially not for Duff. In the third/fourth-place play-off against Ghana 'Blackburn's bionic midget', as the *Sunday Times* described him, provided the assist for Dessie Baker's opener before firing home the winning goal himself.

It capped an excellent few weeks for Duff, and, while they'd been talking about his potential for some time in his home country and in the northwest of England, his showing in Malaysia brought him to the attention of a much wider audience.

In 2003 Duff admitted to the *Sunday Mirror*, 'Until the World Cup last year, the summer of 1997 was the highlight of my international career. It was the tournament that made me. I'll always look back on it with special memories.'

Duff's progress was such that further international recognition was becoming increasingly inevitable. Having given a first-class account of himself at the World Under-20s Championship, he continued to flourish on his return to the domestic game, despite the arrival of another new manager at Ewood Park.

Tony Parkes was in charge only on a temporary basis and, after much speculation linking Sven-Göran Eriksson with the job, the position was eventually taken up by Roy Hodgson, an Englishman relatively unknown in his home country but highly regarded on the Continent following spells with – among others – Malmo, Switzerland and Inter Milan.

The new boss – dubbed 'Roy of the Rovers' by the press – took an immediate liking to Duff and under Hodgson's guidance Blackburn emerged as serious title challengers during the early months of the 1997–8 season, losing just one of their first fifteen Premiership games.

Maintaining that challenge was a test that Hodgson's team

failed to pass, but their final placing of sixth was perfectly respectable – having spent the previous campaign flirting with relegation, Rovers fans could hardly complain.

Duff made a stunning impact during his first full season in the senior side. Aided by the 'surprise' factor that often helps young players through the early stages of their first-team careers, when relatively little is known about them outside the confines of their own club, he emerged as one of the Premiership's most exciting prospects.

In early November he claimed a landmark first goal in senior football. On as a substitute in Blackburn's Premiership clash with Everton at Ewood Park, Duff reacted fastest after Neville Southall had parried Chris Sutton's header to convert the rebound and level the scores at 2–2. Tim Sherwood netted a late winner, and the next day's match report in the *Sunday Times* contained the following line: 'Duff, a deceptively fragile-looking product of Kenny Dalglish's youth policy, not only helped to camouflage his colleagues' defensive weaknesses, but capped a satisfying cameo by claiming his first senior goal.'

The teenage sensation was causing something of a stir, and a few weeks later the *Sun* caught up with him after he'd starred in a 3–1 league win against Bolton.

'I love it at Blackburn,' he said. 'I played for the Irish youth team in Malaysia in the summer so I missed the start of training but Roy Hodgson has been great with me. He works with me and helps me. He tells me to go out there and do my stuff.

'When I was growing up I supported Manchester United and Ryan Giggs was my hero. He made it to the first team when he was 17. I've always looked up to him because he plays in my position. I'm pleased to be in our first-team squad, never mind the team.'

He also pointed out that there was no chance that the considerable attention he was receiving would go to his head. 'Mum and Dad come over when they can,' he added. 'They don't want me to get big-headed and tell me to keep working hard.'

That attention wasn't about to diminish. Duff made sure of that with a series of displays full of raw pace and trickery that brought him a growing band of admirers.

In Blackburn's last game before Christmas, at home to West Ham, he was handed a new role by Hodgson. With Chris Sutton suspended the Rovers boss decided to deploy Duff at centre-forward in the hope that his sharpness would have an unsettling effect at the heart of the visitors' defence.

Using Duff as a makeshift striker would give Blackburn's attack fresh impetus, Hodgson reckoned, with the young Irishman's style contrasting vastly with that of the bigger, more physical target man Sutton.

The plan worked to a T, with Duff scoring twice in a 3–0 win to upstage the two other highly rated teenagers on show that day, West Ham's Rio Ferdinand and Frank Lampard.

Moving Duff into a central attacking position had been a success (as it would be again in the future, particularly at international level), and his Rovers teammates were lining up to voice their agreement after the game.

'Duff was brilliant,' Tim Sherwood told the *Lancashire Evening Telegraph*. 'He gives us a different type of game to what Sutty [Chris Sutton] gives us but he was equally effective. He's class and I bet even Manchester United wish they had him in their squad.'

Stuart Ripley was also impressed. 'Damien was exceptional,' said the England winger. 'He was made for that role. He's only 18 and I don't think even he knows how good he is.'

Another member of the Damien Duff fan club was Jimmy Greaves. In his column in the *Sun*, Greaves paid Duff the ultimate compliment by comparing his playing style to that of the great George Best.

'Blackburn are the most pleasing team on the eye at the moment,' Greaves wrote. 'For those of you unlucky not to have seen George Best play, look at Damien Duff.

'He is in the foothills of his career, but is as important to Blackburn as [Tim] Sherwood and [Chris] Sutton. There will never be another George Best, but you will see glimpses of him in Duff.'

Having made such a telling impact on the Premiership, and having made such a positive impression when representing his country at youth level, the 'Duff for Ireland' bandwagon was gathering pace.

The senior side was going through something of a transitional phase. Jack Charlton had resigned as manager following Ireland's failure to qualify for Euro '96, and his replacement Mick McCarthy had suffered disappointment in his first attempt at leading the team to a major tournament when Ireland narrowly lost to Belgium in a play-off for a place at the 1998 World Cup.

It was time for a change, Irish followers claimed. Not at the helm but on the pitch, where the likes of Ray Houghton, Andy Townsend and Tony Cascarino – each outstanding servants who had long before guaranteed themselves legendary status in Ireland – were all in their mid-thirties and at the very tail end of their international careers. 'Bring in the new' was the cry, with Liam Brady suggesting as much in the *Sunday Times*.

'We've had a great 10 years,' said Brady, in the wake of the Belgium defeat. 'Under Jack Charlton we've been to the last two World Cup finals, but it was always going to be difficult to make it a treble. When we come up against teams from the top drawer the quality is just not there, but that's not to say the situation will stay like that. We've got Damien Duff at Blackburn and Robbie Keane at Wolves, young talent who look likely to come through, so the makings are there for a good European championship campaign.'

If McCarthy had been thinking of injecting his team with new blood, now seemed like the ideal time to do it. And, having responded to questions regarding Duff's possible elevation to the senior side by claiming, 'Nobody appreciates his talent more than I do', the Ireland boss clearly had plans to use the Blackburn youngster before long.

That was indeed the case, and in February 1998 the next stage in Duff's international development saw him named in the Republic of Ireland B team for a meeting with Northern Ireland.

'The level of his performances with Blackburn this season has been very impressive and, while international football is another step higher, I think the lad has the temperament to handle it,' McCarthy told the press. 'That natural talent has to be balanced, of course, against the danger of pushing him too hard, too soon, but hopefully we'll get it right.'

Also playing for Ireland that night was Robbie Keane, a player whom Duff had first come across in a reserve game at Blackburn and someone whose career would draw many parallels with his own.

'I had to ask who he was, so I'd know him the next time,' Duff said of that initial meeting in the *Irish Times*. 'He was taking the mickey out of us all afternoon.'

At just seventeen years old, the impish Wolves striker Keane was the junior member of Ireland's dashing young duo. He'd announced his arrival at club level by scoring twice on his Wolves debut in a 2–0 win at Norwich on the opening day of the season, and big things were expected of him and Duff. In fact, the hype surrounding the two teenagers had grown to an almost unprecedented pitch in Ireland.

Those lofty expectancy levels resulted in masses of fans flocking to Dublin's modest Tolka Park ground for the visit of Northern Ireland. More than ten thousand fans gathered inside the stadium and plenty more were locked out, with estimations of those unable to get in ranging from five hundred to two thousand.

The result didn't go the way of the home side, as Northern Ireland claimed the game's only goal, but, according to McCarthy, 'A lot of people paid to see Robbie Keane and Damien Duff and they didn't disappoint... I've never seen two youngsters of their age group with more talent.'

Someone else impressed by Duff's display was the man Ireland had failed to get the better off at Tolka Park, Northern Ireland goalkeeper Alan Fettis. As a club mate of Duff, Fettis had been aware of his Blackburn colleague's destructive potential for some time, and was perfectly placed to assess his progress.

'For an eighteen-year-old he is incredible,' Fettis told reporters after the game. 'People have been comparing him to George Best but he reminds me more of Chris Waddle. Even at this stage of his development he's got nothing to prove. Damien's got the talent to make an impact at the very highest level. I am not just saying this because he's my teammate at Blackburn, I really believe it.

'He was in a different class in the first half and at the interval our manager Roy Millar said that we had to do something to counteract his ability. We doubled up on him and that helped keep Damien quiet. He was brilliant in that first half and he has a great future ahead of him with club and country. There's no doubt that we'll be hearing an awful lot more about him in the future.'

Although most of the people who'd been in attendance at Tolka Park left the ground singing the praises of Ireland's new star, Duff was far from satisfied with his showing. He couldn't work out what all the fuss was about.

'I was disappointed with my own performance compared with the way I have been playing this season,' Duff told the *Sun*, demonstrating a self-critical tendency that would become a familiar trait. 'It was an opportunity for me to impress, but I'm not sure I did. I know I can do better. At the same time, I enjoyed the occasion.

'I don't know what Mick has in mind for me. As it stands, it's a case of wait and see. Hopefully, though, I will go on to even bigger and better things from here. I didn't get as much of the ball as I like to but, you're not always going to get your own way. Still, at the end of the day, it's another step forward for me.'

Life was definitely changing for Damien Duff. No longer a complete unknown, he was very much part of the Premiership pack and on the brink of full international honours. It was an existence that would take some getting used to.

'This is the first time I have been able to come back to Dublin since the start of the season,' he explained to the *News of the World*, during his return home for the B international.

'Things have been so hectic and it was odd that strangers recognise me in the street now. There has been a lot of pressure this season but it's the kind of pressure I love.'

With a clutch of friendlies on the horizon, prior to the start of Ireland's Euro 2000 qualifying campaign, Duff was hoping that a senior call-up was imminent.

'I'd love to be in the frame for one of those matches,' he said. 'It was great to be named in the side at Tolka Park, but naturally every kid wants to play for his country at the highest level.'

And, on life at Ewood Park, he added, 'It's a big step for a young lad to play in the Premiership, but it's made that much easier when you know that the senior players in the team are looking out for you. People ask if there's pressure for a teenager in the Premiership. Of course there is, but it's the kind of pressure that people my age love.'

The beautiful Czech city of Olomouc, situated almost 300 kilometres east of Prague on the Morava river, does not feature heavily in football's great history. Home to roughly a hundred thousand inhabitants and a little-known team called SK Sigma, the area hardly rivals Madrid or Milan as one of the game's thriving hotbeds. For Damien Duff, though, the place will always occupy a special mark on the timeline of his career.

For it was there that Duff made his senior international debut, on 25 March 1998, in a friendly against the Czech Republic. The match was Ireland's first since they suffered an agonising World Cup play-off defeat at the hands of Belgium four months earlier, and came just twenty-three days after Duff had celebrated his nineteenth birthday.

As predicted, Mick McCarthy used the trip to have a close look at a number of untried players in a largely experimental squad. Despite the inclusion of several new boys, two names were commanding more column inches than any others in the build-up to the game: Damien Duff and Robbie Keane.

Duff's Blackburn colleague Chris Sutton, for example, didn't hold back when evaluating a player who'd been one of the nineteen-goal striker's chief providers that season.

'This kid is the best young talent I have ever seen,' Sutton told the *Mirror*. 'He is easily the best player for his age I have come across and already I would rate him ahead of Ryan Giggs. Damien is going to be a great player for Ireland.'

In McCarthy's pre-match address to the media, the Ireland boss also spoke glowingly of the Rovers man, before contradicting himself somewhat by urging everyone to – well, to stop speaking glowingly of the Rovers man.

'I have no fears for Damien,' he said. 'In fact, he will only get better with age. He's a smashing lad. His attitude is amazing. For a nineteen-year-old, he's incredibly mature. The sky's the limit for Damien. He plays off the cuff, which is what makes him so exciting. He's such a special talent. A lot of players will come and go in the next ten years or so but you can be sure Damien will still be here.

'We can all see that Damien has got the lot – great first touch, pace, control and finishing ability. He is also a deceptively strong athlete. But when he made his first appearance for the Irish B side last month he was very disappointed with his performance and he thought it was a lot to do with all the expectations put upon him. Let's just give him some space and see how he plays. Then if you want you can rave about him then.'

Eager to shield Duff from the press, McCarthy added, 'I'll let Damien talk to you after he's scored a goal and showed us all why he's being compared to Ryan Giggs and George Best.'

In a game that saw McCarthy hand debuts to six members of his young squad – Duff, seventeen-year-old Keane, Mark Kinsella, Alan Maybury, Graham Kavanagh and Rory Delap – Duff didn't get that goal, but he did do enough in his seventy-two-minute appearance to justify the pre-match hype.

'He's only a lad, still making his way in the game, and it's wrong to start making comparisons with older, very gifted players,' said McCarthy afterwards. 'But, yes, Damien is a player who excites crowds. People still love to see wingers take on full backs and go past them and Damien certainly did that against the Czechs.'

Ireland lost the match 2–1, which was by no means a disgrace against a decent Czech outfit, and reporters reserved special praise for one particular debutant.

The *Irish Times* said: 'Damien Duff's first-half performance contained at least half-a-dozen flashes of his enormous potential… Everything about him suggests a special career ahead.'

Meanwhile, the *Sunday Mirror* stated: 'The walk was different and the blond hair was certainly a million miles removed from the original Beatle-cut. But there were times in Olomouc when Blackburn teenager Damien Duff impressed the crowd as the new George Best… at 19, it was a stunning debut by the Dubliner.'

Duff's natural shyness means that he's always felt uncomfortable when confronted by the press, and this occasion was no different. The old cliché about players who prefer to do their talking on the pitch can rarely have been more appropriate, and Duff was happy to leave the post-match analysis to everyone else in Olomouc.

He did, however, share his memories of the experience with the *Irish Times* a few years later. 'It was great,' he said. 'I remember having a tear in my eye when the anthem was played and then the game was great. My job is going past people and I suppose back then I thought I'd have to beat people all day. I was trying to be Billy the Hero, but I was just a young lad and it was a great honour. I played about 70 minutes that day and hoped to build on that.'

During Duff's early days in the senior Ireland squad he suddenly found himself training alongside players he'd idolised as a child, and by his own admission he felt star-struck in the company of Steve Staunton, Denis Irwin, Roy Keane, Niall Quinn and Tony Cascarino – all members of Big Jack's famous World Cup brigade.

Shortly after Duff completed his move to Chelsea in 2003, the veteran striker Cascarino recalled his first impressions of the slight teenager in *The Times*. 'When I first saw Damien Duff in training with Ireland, I thought he looked like some sort of strange cartoon character – a sort of badly drawn boy,' he said. 'A spindly lad, with baggy shorts hanging off him, he appeared far too small and frail to be a club player, let alone an international. Surely, he would be brushed off the ball too easily. He loped along with an awkward pace that we soon discovered belied his fluency on the ball. During a five-a-side, he whizzed around seasoned defenders, made a mockery of players and nut-megged Denis Irwin. He was so confident in his ability, and being young and naïve, he played without fear. He was the talk of the dressing room.'

Cascarino also revealed that Duff's dietary habits left a lot to be desired back then. He remembered how, soon after joining the squad, Duff once devoured a traditional Irish breakfast of eggs, bacon, sausages and beans while his teammates 'watched the food swirling around his wide-open mouth like a washing machine'. Cascarino also recalled another occasion when, on the day of a match, he saw a waiter taking a tray of scones – accompanied by a large dollop of jam and cream – to a room occupied by Duff and Robbie Keane. 'If Mick McCarthy had found out, he would have been far from pleased,' wrote Cascarino. 'But Duff would say: "No problem, carbohydrates." '

CHAPTER 4

Growing Pains

'Roy Hodgson said to me that your second year will always
be your hardest. I know now how right he was.'

DAMIEN DUFF, MARCH 2001

To say that life was treating Damien Duff pretty well as
his maiden first-team campaign came to a close is
something of an understatement. The teenager was
appearing regularly in the Premiership, was earning rave
reviews from all quarters and could look forward to testing
himself in Europe after Rovers' sixth-place finish had
guaranteed them a UEFA Cup spot. He was also a full
international *and* he'd bagged a megabucks sponsorship deal
with Adidas. It seemed as though things couldn't get much
better. They would eventually, but only after first taking a
frustrating turn for the worse.

In brief, the 1998–9 season was hugely disappointing for
Blackburn Rovers and for Duff. The Lancashire club failed
miserably to build on Roy Hodgson's promising debut year
by starting the campaign in such dreadful fashion that the

manager was sacked and replaced by Alex Ferguson's assistant at Manchester United, Brian Kidd.

Bringing in someone who was highly respected as a number two but whose managerial experience amounted to an unremarkable spell at nonleague Barrow and a handful of games in charge of Fourth Division Preston in the mid-1980s represented a massive gamble by Rovers' millionaire owner Jack Walker. Ultimately, it was one that didn't pay off, as Blackburn dropped out of the Premiership just four years after winning it.

For Duff it was a harsh lesson, an abrupt reminder that, in football, fortunes can change in an instant. His second full season was always going to be hard, anyway. Without the advantage of being an unknown quantity he was sure to find that opposing teams would be devising specific ways to stop him; almost every teenager who bursts onto the scene with such vigour subsequently suffers from some degree of 'second-season syndrome'.

But Duff's case was exasperated by other factors. First of all, he'd spent the summer recovering from surgery to cure a hernia problem that had been troubling him for some time.

'I found it a pain for quite a long time, about four months in fact,' he later said in the *Mirror*. 'Sometimes it would be bad, it would just nag, and it's hard to concentrate with a bad pain, so I was glad to get into the hospital and have the operation.'

In addition to that the whole team was struggling to find any sort of form, a new manager failed to bring out the best in him and his club campaign was disrupted further when he spent the bulk of April in Nigeria with Ireland for the World Under-20s

Championship. His form was duly affected, and it wasn't only at club level that the going became increasingly tough.

Ireland were grouped with Croatia, Yugoslavia, Macedonia and Malta for the Euro 2000 qualifiers and began their campaign with a home fixture against Croatia in September 1998. Miroslav Blazevic's highly competent outfit had surprised everyone by finishing third at the World Cup, and even without the injured Davor Suker – the man who'd scooped the golden boot in France that summer – the visitors were sure to provide Mick McCarthy's men with as serious a test as almost anyone.

So McCarthy's decision to include Duff in his starting line-up gave a clear indication of the manager's unstinting belief in his rookie winger. Having followed up his debut in the Czech Republic by winning a second cap against Mexico, Duff would be making only his third senior international appearance and his first in a competitive match.

The day evoked mixed emotions for the Blackburn man. Ireland won 2–0 to get their qualifying campaign off to a flyer, but Duff was withdrawn at half-time as McCarthy brought on full-back Jeff Kenna to help protect his team's two-goal advantage.

Duff retained his place in the team for Ireland's next qualifier, though, at home to Malta less than six weeks later. It was another learning experience for Duff, who was beginning to find himself with more than just one defender for company whenever he was in possession of the ball. It provided the nineteen-year-old with a challenge he would have to overcome if he was to satisfy his international ambitions. According to his manager, he would have no problems in doing just that.

'I thought Damien did OK,' said McCarthy after the game. 'It's a big step up and very often they got two players on him and made it hard for him. But he did well. I'm pleased with him and he's learning all the time. He bypassed under-21s football and came straight into this level and he's coped well. He's got a bright future.'

Although Duff made a respectable start to his international career, his impact had been overshadowed by the exploits of Robbie Keane. Against Malta, Keane scored twice to become Ireland's youngest ever goalscorer, breaking a record that Johnny Giles had held for almost forty years.

Duff was handed an opportunity to redress the balance the following month when Ireland travelled to Yugoslavia for a match that had initially been scheduled for October but was postponed due to the political unrest in Belgrade (a situation that would continue to hamper Ireland's quest for a place at Euro 2000 throughout the qualifying phase).

The conflict in the Balkans had delayed the start of Yugoslavia's campaign, so, by the time Group 8 leaders Ireland arrived in Belgrade, the excited state of the home supporters had reached fever pitch. Duff, though, was unperturbed by the prospect of a hostile atmosphere.

'It's probably the biggest match I've been involved in,' he told the press before the game. 'The stadium is huge and it will be full. But I'm not bothered. I'm just looking forward to the match and, hopefully, we can come away from it with a result.

'My confidence is grand. I feel I've been playing well at club level. But you don't get noticed as much when the team's struggling. Hopefully, I can do the business because Mick has shown a lot of faith in me. I know I'm good enough to be given this chance.'

Come matchday the atmosphere inside the Red Star stadium was every bit as intimidating as Ireland had expected. McCarthy's men refused to buckle but, despite a determined effort, the visitors came away empty-handed after losing to a solitary Predrag Mijatovic goal.

Duff felt the pain of defeat as much as anyone, although he was able to take comfort from the quality of his own performance. Playing wide left in a 4–5–1 formation, he gave a classic display of positive wing play that delighted his boss.

'Duffer was excellent,' McCarthy announced to the press after the game. 'I'm delighted for him. That's the best he's played for us. I've told him that, told him he's done well. He is a very good player. You'd never have guessed, from the way he took on players with track records as long as your arm, that here was a lad, just gone nineteen and playing only his fifth international game.

'Some felt that perhaps he hadn't played as well as he might have against Croatia – that he still has some way to go to make it on the biggest stage of all. I just hope they were looking in on this game. He showed time and again why he's rated as one of the best of the up-and-coming players in the Premiership.

'Take it from one who's been around a long time – there are few tougher tests in international football than a game against Yugoslavia in their own back yard. The atmosphere in the stadium was intimidating at best. But he took it all in his stride. The fact that two Yugoslavs were booked trying to stop him said it all.'

Duff also expressed his satisfaction. 'I was pleased,' he said. 'Things are getting easier for me match by match. I thought it was the best performance I've had.'

True to form, Duff continued a turbulent campaign when he returned to Ewood Park. A 2–0 defeat at home to fellow strugglers Southampton left Blackburn planted at the foot of the Premiership, and Roy Hodgson was shown the door barely six months after guiding the club to a top-six finish.

Ironically, it was Hodgson who had warned Duff of the potential perils he would face after enjoying such an impressive debut season.

In an interview with the *Sunday Times* in March 2001, Duff remembered his former manager's advice. 'Roy said to me that your second year will always be your hardest. I know now how right he was. He told me I'd probably have a couple of players marking me and I still get it now even away from home. It's something you get used to.'

While the exiting manager clearly appreciated Duff's qualities the new man at the helm was not, it transpired, such a big fan.

Duff played the full ninety minutes of Brian Kidd's first game in charge – a 1–0 victory over Charlton at the beginning of December – but started the next five games on the bench. Kidd obviously felt that Blackburn's perilous position called for hard graft and experience, and on the left-hand side of midfield that meant a place for the seasoned Jason Wilcox instead of the precocious Duff.

Even when he did finally get a start, against Leeds in January, he was replaced after just twenty-five minutes as Kidd made a tactical switch in response to the sending-off of Tim Sherwood. And that wasn't the only time that Duff paid the price for Blackburn's poor disciplinary record. When Rovers travelled to Chelsea later that season he was introduced as an eightieth-minute substitute, only to be hauled off before the end following the dismissal of centre-half Marlon Broomes. It was an embarrassing episode in an increasingly frustrating club campaign for Duff.

At least Mick McCarthy still loved him. The Ireland boss stayed loyal to the youngster and was rewarded with a brilliant individual display in Ireland's 2–0 friendly win against Paraguay in February.

In the *Irish Times*, former Ireland defender Mark Lawrenson said, 'Again, Damien Duff showed his pedigree. Paraguay play extremely deep, a typically South American style, and that suited the Blackburn lad, it gave him an extra yard or two of space he won't normally see at international level. But he just raced through what ground he was shown and whipped in some devilish crosses. That ability he has to simply breeze by opponents is priceless at this level. I'm sure he has already raised a few eyebrows among other managers in the Irish qualifying group. His continuing development has to please McCarthy greatly.'

The *Mirror* claimed: 'Damien Duff launched a left wing revolution at Lansdowne Road last night. Denis Irwin and

David Connolly provided the goals – but it was Duff who provided the inspiration. In only his sixth appearance in the green shirt, Damien proved a bad omen for the visiting South Americans as he weaved dazzling patterns down the tramlines.'

Equally impressed were his teammates. Kenny Cunningham told a gathering of reporters after the match, 'That was one of the best games Damien's had in an Irish shirt. We all know how tough South American defenders can be, but he looked threatening whenever he had the ball. He was exhilarating at times. And that's exactly what we need – high-quality crosses – if we're to take advantage of Niall Quinn's strength in the air.

'It's easy to forget Damien's tender age and to find himself in international football when he's still so young must be a daunting task. But he's going to get better and better. I still don't think we've seen the best of him.'

Captain Roy Keane also chipped in. 'It was a superb performance by Damien,' he said. 'Sometimes in matches like these players hold back, but that wasn't the case with Damien. He sent over some fine crosses and thoroughly deserved the man-of-the-match award.'

At the end of March, as Blackburn's fight for survival entered a critical phase, Duff headed for Africa, not to escape the misery of playing a bit-part role in his club's slide towards relegation, but to represent his country at the World Under-20s Championship. Two years earlier, the same competition had provided Duff with a springboard from which he launched his career by scoring a couple of memorable goals to help Ireland claim a third-place finish.

This time round the tournament was riddled with controversy. Playing it in Nigeria raised serious health-and-safety fears, but the most contentious issue concerned its timing. Whereas the 1997 event in Malaysia was held in the off-season months of June and July, the tournament had now been moved to April. FIFA insisted that clubs accept all call-ups, and the decision caused outrage among those forced to make do without key players at a crucial time of the campaign.

Many regarded the tournament as nothing more than a disruption to the domestic season. Duff, just twenty years old and eligible for Brian Kerr's squad even though he'd been capped six times at senior level, did not agree. He'd already made his senior debut at Blackburn by the time of the 1997 tournament but, he argued, it was only after his starring display in Malaysia that Roy Hodgson had begun to take serious notice of him.

'People are entitled to their opinions but in my case the last under-20 championship was the making of me,' Duff told the *News of the World*. 'I learned a lot by playing in different conditions and against players who had new ideas on the game. I think I grew up more in those four weeks than I had in two seasons at Blackburn. And I believe a lot of Irish players are going to be saying the same thing when they get back from Nigeria.

'Nobody likes being away from their clubs at such an important time in the season. In my case, I've had to work hard to stay in the frame at Ewood Park and I'd love to be still there when they're fighting for vital Premiership survival points. But hopefully I'll come back from Africa a better player – and in the long run that can only help the club.'

Just as he had done two years earlier, Duff scored twice in the tournament. It wasn't enough, however, to help his team emulate the boys of '97. In stifling heat, Ireland lost to Mexico in their opening game but beat Saudi Arabia (2–0) and Australia (4–0) to clinch a place in the knockout phase. Duff scored in both of those victories but couldn't stop Ireland from going out of the competition to Nigeria, on penalties, in the second round.

The result left Duff devastated. 'I don't know why we didn't do so well in Nigeria,' he later reflected in the *Irish Times*. 'The heat was a big thing. Getting knocked out over there was the only time I remember coming in from a match and crying. It looked like we had a great team there. I really thought we'd do it.'

Dejected by Ireland's failure to progress beyond the last sixteen in Nigeria, Duff returned to Lancashire looking for some sort of pick-me-up. Unfortunately for him, that was the last thing he was likely to find at Ewood Park.

He did manage to open his account for the season, but even that was in a 3–1 defeat at home to Liverpool. The rot had well and truly set in, and, after winning just one of their final fourteen matches, Blackburn were relegated.

Rovers' fate was officially sealed after they drew 0–0 at home to Manchester United in their penultimate game, although the writing had been on the wall for some time before that. The arrival of Brian Kidd had failed to inject fresh impetus into an ailing campaign, even though Jack Walker had funded a spending spree that saw the new manager bring Keith Gillespie, Ashley Ward, Matt Jansen, Jason McAteer and Lee Carsley to the club for a sum of almost £20 million.

Kidd's frustrations boiled over after watching his team lose 2–1 at home to an already relegated Nottingham Forest side that played the second half at Ewood Park with ten men. With two games remaining, the result left Rovers staring relegation in the face, and Kidd decided it was time to let rip at his charges.

'The players looked frightened to death and didn't want it enough,' he ranted in his post-match press conference. 'A lot of them are rubber dinghy men, the ship is going down but they're all saying, "I'll go for help" – and that's why you've got to question their courage. Brave men can have bad games and I can live with that, but today there was no courage. People are hiding...'

Ireland began the 1999–2000 season with unfinished business to sort out, and, while his fortunes may have dipped at club level, Duff was still a part of Mick McCarthy's plans for Euro 2000 qualification.

After Ireland beat Macedonia 1–0 those plans were disrupted when, for the second time in the campaign, politics intervened and one of Ireland's qualifiers was called off at short notice. This time it was a home match with Yugoslavia, originally scheduled for June but moved instead to September after the Irish government refused to issue visas to the visitors' travelling party in protest at the atrocities being carried out at the time by the Yugoslav regime.

Rumours that Ireland would lose points, be fined or have to play the match at a neutral venue proved to be just talk, and the match finally went ahead at Lansdowne Road. Ireland won 2–1, without the injured Duff, to make it four wins out of five qualifiers. Their hopes of claiming top spot in Group 8 were tempered by a 1–0 defeat in Croatia (a game that Duff started), but a tense 3–2 victory away to Malta (when Duff came on as a substitute) left them in decent shape ahead of their final qualifier in Macedonia.

In yet another rearranged fixture, against the second-weakest team in the group, Ireland went into the match knowing that a win would guarantee them at least a play-off place, and would see them qualify automatically as winners of the section if Yugoslavia failed to beat Croatia in the day's other Group 8 encounter.

As it turned out, Yugoslavia did fail to beat Croatia, managing just a 2–2 draw in Zagreb. That left the door open for Ireland to claim a prized place at the finals but, after suffering the most devastating of late blows, Mick McCarthy's men failed to take full advantage. Leading through Niall Quinn's first-half goal, they were seconds away from sealing the necessary victory in Skopje when the home side grabbed an equaliser following an injury-time corner. For the third major tournament in succession, the dreaded play-offs beckoned for Ireland.

Duff watched the whole agonising event unfold from the bench in Macedonia and played no part in the game. As his hangover from Blackburn's disastrous relegation campaign continued, his slide down the pecking order at club level was now being mirrored in the international setup as well, with Mark Kennedy, Kevin Kilbane and Rory Delap all preferred to the Rovers man in the wide positions.

He was once again among the substitutes when Ireland faced Turkey in the play-offs – hardly an ideal draw for McCarthy's men, especially as many had been hoping for a clash closer to home against either England or Scotland. Knowing that a vociferous welcome was awaiting them in the away leg, Ireland set out to establish an advantage in the opening game at Lansdowne Road and were on course to get it after Robbie Keane broke the deadlock just eleven minutes from the end.

Moments later, however, the visitors claimed a priceless away goal when Tayfur drew them level from the penalty spot. It was a hammer blow, and one from which Ireland never recovered. The return match, played in front of a partisan home crowd in Bursa, was drawn 0–0 and Turkey progressed to the finals on the away-goals rule.

What made Ireland's exit harder to stomach was the conduct of the hosts. At the final whistle Tony Cascarino was offered a handshake by opponent Beserler Ali Eren, but, because the defender had, according to Cascarino, 'spent the previous ten minutes spitting at me', the striker understandably declined the invitation. The Turkish player then attempted to trip Cascarino, the Irishman responded with a sharp verbal blast and all hell broke loose.

Duff appeared as a substitute in Bursa, as he had done in

the first leg, but it was Cascarino who later revealed details of the ugly post-match brawl in *The Times*. He wrote,

> Kevin Kilbane, Gary Breen and Roy Keane were involved while Damien Duff left the pitch holding the back of his head. We had no protection. Hundreds of armed police rushed on to the pitch and waded in as fists flew among the players. Eventually, my face blooded, I walked down the tunnel and protested to a policeman about the treatment. He just turned his back and ignored me. One of the Turkey players stood in the tunnel and, gesturing to me, ran his fingers across his throat as if he wanted to cut it... I've never played anywhere like it – it was a septic cauldron of hatred.

Despite the £10 million sale of Chris Sutton to Chelsea, the playing roster at Ewood Park still contained enough quality for bookies to install Blackburn as red-hot favourites for promotion in the summer of 1999. Making an instant return to the Premiership wouldn't be straightforward, though, as Duff was quick to point out.

> No disrespect to any of the clubs in the Nationwide First Division, but I reckon it's going to be a bit of a culture shock after the Premiership,' he said in the *Sunday Mirror*. He continued: 'Like a lot of other relegated teams in the past, we felt despite our disappointing results in the games that mattered, we were too good to go down. But the time for self-pity is

over. Now we must prove that we have the skill and – just as important – the character to get ourselves back among the big boys again. And we will.

Encouragingly for Duff, who up to that point had been used only sparingly by Brian Kidd, the manager offered some reassuring words as the new season approached.

'I've always rated Damien even before I came to Ewood Park and, despite so many things going wrong last season, nothing changed my mind about that,' said Kidd. 'Not only is he quick and skilful, but he's a good competitor. And we're going to need all those qualities over the next nine months.'

There were several qualities required to initiate an immediate bounce-back in form at Ewood Park but, whatever they were, Rovers struggled to find them. Having coped poorly with the pressure induced by a relegation dogfight in the previous campaign, Blackburn had even more trouble coping with the pressure of being title favourites.

They made an awful start to the new season – losing to Huddersfield, Barnsley and Swindon, and scraping draws against Grimsby and Walsall is hardly the form of a championship-winning outfit. At the back end of October QPR won 2–0 at Ewood Park to consign Rovers to a seventh straight league game without a win, and leave the 1995 Premiership champions just two points above the First Division drop zone.

Home supporters made their feelings known at the final whistle with a barrage of jeers, but no one felt the frustration more than Jack Walker. He decided that the only way to put the brakes on his club's alarming slide down the league ladder was once again to change the man in charge and, eleven months after arriving at Ewood Park, Brian Kidd was ushered through the exit door.

Picking up the pieces in the wake of Kidd's departure was a man who'd become accustomed to assuming such a role over the years, assistant boss Tony Parkes, and news of that move was most definitely music to the ears of Damien Duff. Parkes had given Duff his senior debut during a previous reign as caretaker manager and the young Irishman's prospects of regaining a first-team place were instantly boosted.

Parkes inspired an immediate turnaround, as Rovers lost just one of their next fifteen games in all competitions to launch, belatedly, a surge towards the top six. The club had rediscovered a winning habit and Duff as much as anyone was revelling in the new man's stewardship.

In Parkes's second game in charge, when Fulham were the visitors to Ewood Park, Duff set up the opening goal for Egil Ostenstad and claimed the second himself in a vital 2–0 win.

'Duff hasn't had the happiest of seasons at Blackburn, but Brian Kidd's departure would appear to have given him a new lease of life,' reckoned the *Irish Times*.

From there he continued to impress. Unlike his predecessor Kidd, Parkes handed Duff a regular role in the side and was rewarded with a string of excellent displays by a winger who was once again playing with real freedom and confidence. Duff's impact was such that in December Parkes sanctioned the sale to Leeds United of Jason Wilcox, a player who had long been Duff's chief rival for a place on the left-hand side

A youthful Damien playing for Ireland against Ghana in the World Youth Championship in the summer of 1997 at the age of 18.

That soon-to-be-famous left peg in action as a schoolboy international.

Above: A precocious talent, Damien's skill was evident whenever he went near a football.

Below: A keen all-round sportsman, Damien makes the most of his spare time during the U-20s World Championship by practising his putting in the team hotel.

Above left: Kenny Dalglish guided Blackburn to the Premiership title in 1994-95 and also recruited the fledgling talent of Duff.

Above right: Pat Devlin, a key figure in Irish talent-spotting and the man who alerted Dalglish to Damien's burgeoning reputation.

Below: Brian Kidd in December 1998. Duff's form, and his relationship with Kidd – his fourth boss at Blackburn – was less successful than with other club managers.

As a lad, one of Duff's footballing heroes was Kevin Sheedy, the former Everton and Ireland left-sided midfielder. In the 1-1 draw against England in Italia '90 (above) Sheedy's equaliser sparked an unforgettable tournament for the Irish.

Duff demonstrates the speed, poise and skill that made him one of the game's most potent forwards during his time at Blackburn. Here he drifts past Tottenham's Chris Perry in the 2002 Worthington Cup final (below).

Above left: Roy Keane in typical sturdy captain mode. His outburst at the World Cup in 2002 threatened to overshadow Ireland's performance at the competition.

Above right: Mick McCarthy reflects on things prior to the first group match against Cameroon.

Below: A tired-looking Duff awaits the press in Japan.

Above: In local style, Duff celebrates scoring a goal against Saudi Arabia in Ireland's group E victory in Yokohama, before Robbie Keane arrives to join in.

Below: Duff and team-mates look dejected after they are narrowly beaten on penalties by Spain in the second round. Duff didn't take a spot-kick – 'My one great regret,' he would later admit.

of the Blackburn midfield.

Duff was grateful for the vote of confidence. 'I was in and out under Brian Kidd and I just wanted to get in the team,' he admitted to the *Sun*. 'But since he's gone, Tony Parkes has shown confidence in me and it's been great to be back in the team. It's great to be playing again. I don't mean to boast, but I'm happy with the way I'm playing. For the last couple of seasons Jason Wilcox and I have been fighting for that spot and at the end of the day one of us had to go. It could have been me, but the club decided to sell Jason to Leeds.'

At the beginning of the new millennium, Blackburn and Duff were in pretty good shape. They were now being talked about as serious play-off contenders – a claim that was substantiated by a 1–0 FA Cup fourth-round win away to Liverpool, in which Duff was superb – and their nightmare start to the season was firmly behind them.

Parkes was pleased with the contribution that the revitalised Duff had made to that run. 'Damien has returned to the kind of form he displayed in his first season for Blackburn in the Premiership and the fans love it,' he told the press. 'He's been outstanding these past few weeks and, against Liverpool, it was impossible for any defender to catch him. The good thing is that he's still so young. And as he gains more experience, particularly on the international scene, he's only going to get better.

'He's developed a lot this year and is far stronger. At times I used to look at him after ten minutes and think he should be sitting alongside me. He's very much like Chris Waddle – he looks knackered, but then the ball comes to his feet and he is away.'

Duff's resurgence had not gone unnoticed by other managers either. Huddersfield's Steve Bruce claimed that Duff was 'the best left-sided player in the division', after watching him terrorise his side in Rovers' 2–0 victory at Ewood Park, while Duff's international boss had also been impressed. Although his Ireland career had lost a little momentum in recent months, it was comforting to know that Mick McCarthy had not lost faith in the Ballyboden boy.

'Look at our available left-sided midfielders and you appreciate just how competitive the position is,' said McCarthy. 'Apart from Damien, I have the choice of Kevin Kilbane and Mark Kennedy, both of whom did exceptionally well last year. Then there's Keith O'Neill. These days, I tend to view him as a front player, but he's equally at home playing wide on the left. From a manager's point of view, that's a healthy situation... but Damien knows that, when he's playing well, he's always going to be in the frame.'

It was clear for all to see that Duff had overcome the problems that had blighted his second season in senior football. He was enjoying himself again and for that, he felt, the new man at the helm deserved great credit.

'The training hasn't changed much under "Tone" but everybody gets on with him,' Duff told the *Daily Mail*.

'He has been here for years, we all know and like him and that really helps when you are trying to win matches. He is much easier to get on with than Brian Kidd. We have always called him "Tone". With Kidd, it was "boss".

'I suppose I am just playing with more confidence now and

it helps that I am in the team every week. I wasn't confident under Brian Kidd but I am now. I think we all had confidence problems at the start of the season but now we are flying.'

Just as talk of making the play-offs began to circulate around Ewood Park, Blackburn were brought down to earth with a considerable bump when they travelled to Yorkshire to face Barnsley and were dealt a 5–1 thrashing. An FA Cup exit at the hands of Newcastle soon followed, and a run of one point from twelve in the league seriously hurt Rovers' promotion ambitions.

In the meantime, Blackburn continued their search for a manager – Parkes had done a fine job, but his brief had always been to mind the shop until a new boss could be installed. In March that search ended with the capture of Graeme Souness. 'Anybody in football would have found this job hard to turn down,' said a man who included stints at Rangers, Liverpool, Galatasaray, Southampton, Torino and Benfica on his managerial CV.

For Duff it was a case of 'another season, another manager'. Since arriving in Lancashire five years earlier he had seen Kenny Dalglish, Ray Harford, Roy Hodgson, Brian Kidd and Tony Parkes swap places in the Blackburn hot seat. And he'd only just turned twenty-one. Now it was the turn of Souness to rouse the Rovers.

Although the club still harboured ambitions of making a late run into the play-offs – ambitions that were bolstered by a 5–0 home demolition of Sheffield United, in which Duff scored twice – Rovers failed to win any of their last six matches and dropped out of contention.

Duff carried on performing under Souness exactly as he had done under Parkes. The player some reporters had labelled the 'Comeback Kid' finished the season in such dazzling style that he scooped the club's Player of the Year award and, crucially, also earned himself the respect of his new boss.

'A lot of encouraging things have been happening at the club in the last month and Damien's contribution is one of them,' Souness said in the *Sunday Mirror*. 'He's always had great ability and the vision and the skill to take on defenders. But there are times when all young players – even the best of them – run low on confidence. Now he's got it back. And I reckon that's beginning to rub off on the rest of the team.'

Blackburn goalkeeper Alan Kelly was in agreement, explaining Duff's influence on the team in the most precise terms. 'Damien's been brilliant – our man of the match in six of the last nine games,' he said. 'There isn't a better winger in the First Division just now... and he's doing it on a consistent basis.'

Not for the last time in his career, rumours linking Duff with a move away from Blackburn began to emerge. Duff reacted by pledging his allegiance to the club in emphatic fashion.

'I can't wait for next season,' he told the *Lancashire Evening Telegraph*. 'A new manager has come in and he hasn't said much yet, but I want to be part of things. I suppose we messed up at the start of the season this year and everything has stemmed from that really... But if we can get a good start next season, I don't see why we should not go straight back up. I love Blackburn, it's the only place for me

– a true blue.'

The most prominent of those rumours suggested that a switch to Bobby Robson's Newcastle was on the cards, but Souness was adamant that Duff would be going nowhere. Also speaking to the *Lancashire Evening Telegraph*, he said, 'Newcastle would not be alone in wanting Damien Duff but Damien Duff is not for sale. Bobby Robson did phone and Damien's name cropped up but managers talk all the time and Damien's name is often the first they mention. However, Damien is happy at Blackburn Rovers. He wants to get back in the Premier League and we want to get there together. So as far as I'm concerned he is going nowhere for many, many years.'

The matter was effectively closed in June 2000, when Blackburn announced that Duff had signed a new four-year contract.

'Great times lie ahead at Ewood Park,' he said. 'It's my club and I've always been happy here. Our job now is to get us back where we belong, in the Premiership.'

Souness was relieved to see the issue resolved. 'Damien is a young player with enormous talent and it's around a player like him that the club's future depends,' he said.

CHAPTER 5

Far Eastern Promise

'I believe real heroes are people who fight
in wars and die for their country, but in football
terms they are all heroes for me.'

MICK McCARTHY, NOVEMBER 2001

Mick McCarthy could have been forgiven for thinking the gods were conspiring against him as he prepared to begin his third attempt at guiding Ireland to the finals of a major tournament as the summer of 2000 drew to a close. His previous two efforts had seen the team miss out in the most agonising fashion, with play-off defeats against Belgium and then Turkey denying them a place at the finals of the 1998 World Cup and Euro 2000.

So, with Ireland's last appearance among the game's elite – at the World Cup in 1994 – slipping ever distantly into the past, McCarthy was desperate to test his young side on the grandest of stages by securing a spot at the 2002 World Cup finals in Japan & South Korea.

It wasn't going to be easy, of course, and the draw for the qualifying phase gave a stark reminder of that. Three of

Group 2's six teams – Estonia, Cyprus and Andorra – were never expected to claim either the first automatic qualifying spot or the play-off consolation offered by a second-place finish (although, with memories of a 0–0 Euro '96 qualifying draw against Liechtenstein still fresh in Irish minds, taking maximum points from that trio of outsiders could hardly have been considered straightforward).

The other two teams in the group would provide the sternest of tests, though. In Holland and Portugal, Ireland would be in competition with two of international football's most potent outfits, each fresh from semi-finals appearances at the recent European Championships.

What's more, Ireland's first two fixtures were away – in Holland and then Portugal. If McCarthy and his men were going to fulfil their World Cup dream, they would have to do it the hard way. As if that were not challenging enough, two members of the Irish squad decided to heap further pressure on the boss by virtue of a comical incident that the *Irish Times* sensationally termed 'the biggest scandal involving the national team in almost 75 years of competition'.

With their opening match away to Holland approaching on the Saturday, McCarthy had gathered his squad in Dublin and was happy to see them head into town for a few 'relaxing' drinks on the Monday night.

By 3.45 a.m. on the Tuesday, Phil Babb and Mark Kennedy were extremely relaxed. So much so that the pair were arrested and charged with being drunk in public, a breach of the peace and causing criminal damage following a series of high jinks that culminated in Babb launching himself onto a police car that, unfortunately for the Sporting Lisbon defender, was parked outside a police station at the time. The fact that Babb later admitted to 'sliding across the bonnet of the car Starsky-and-Hutch-style' merely added to the farce.

McCarthy, though, was not amused. Having woken to the news that two of his players had spent the night in police cells just days before the start of their World Cup qualifying campaign, he later attended Dublin's District Court as the embarrassed pair were released on bail.

He then hauled both players into a press conference and announced his own course of action: Phil Babb and Mark Kennedy would play no part against Holland, and were banished from the squad immediately with serious question marks placed against their international futures.

But it wasn't all bad for the Irish, not least for Damien Duff. The absence of Kennedy suddenly left Duff in a two-way race with Kevin Kilbane for a starting place on the left-hand side of the Ireland midfield.

And, it seemed, this wasn't a bad time to be facing the Dutch. Still nursing a hangover from their Euro 2000 semi-final defeat at the hands of Italy just two months beforehand, new coach Louis van Gaal had a depleted squad to choose from himself, not due to any Starsky-and-Hutch-style antics but because of injuries, with key players Jaap Stam, Edgar Davids, Marc Overmars and Boudewijn Zenden all among those on the sick list.

Just to add a little more spice to the build-up, defender Michael Reiziger used his website to announce that Holland were making plans to ensure an early exit for Roy Keane:

If we're smart we could get him a red card because he has a dodgy temperament. If referees know that about a player they are always far more likely to card them. We will have to provoke Keane in some way. Perhaps holding his shirt or walking in to him after he passes the ball. Players are also known to whisper comments about another player's mother or the size of parts of his body. I don't like that side of the game very much but if it helps us to win then it's worthwhile.

Needless to say, McCarthy was a relieved man when the game finally got under way in the Amsterdam Arena. Sixty-five minutes later that relief had turned to unexpected joy after Robbie Keane showed just why Inter Milan had recently parted with £13 million for his services by opening the scoring and then setting up Jason McAteer to give Ireland a 2–0 lead.

The home side rallied, and late goals from Jeffrey Talan and Giovanni van Bronckhorst earned Holland a 2–2 draw. But, all things considered, Ireland could hardly be disappointed with a point.

Duff, meanwhile, watched the whole game from the bench as McCarthy opted to replace the exiled Kennedy with Kilbane. It was becoming a familiar situation for Duff, forced into a bit-part role at the expense of an industrious winger who was revelling in Sunderland's surprising success in the Premiership.

Blackburn's continued absence from the top flight was hardly helping Duff's cause and it came as no surprise when

McCarthy named an unchanged line-up for the second of Ireland's qualifiers, against Portugal in Lisbon, the following month.

It was another tough test for the visitors but, once again, they emerged unbeaten. After watching the excellent Luis Figo and Rui Costa dictate events for long periods, Ireland salvaged a 1–1 draw and another vital point, thanks to substitute Matt Holland's long-range leveller.

At the heart of the move that led to Holland's strike was another substitute – Damien Duff. Introduced in place of Jason McAteer midway through the second half, Duff made a decent impression in his first ever World Cup appearance. 'Duff injected life into the Irish midfield,' said the *Mirror*.

That impressive cameo led some reporters to suggest that Duff may have done enough to earn a starting place for the visit of Estonia to Lansdowne Road four days later, especially as Robbie Keane – who spent the second half in Lisbon playing as a lone striker – himself admitted that the extra support offered by the introduction of his old pal had made his job considerably easier. But McCarthy remained loyal to the starting XI that had earned such positive results in Ireland's opening two matches, and again named an unchanged side.

So, once again, no starting role for Duff. But he did come on to replace McAteer, and was allowed the whole of the second half to patrol the right wing as goals from Mark Kinsella and Richard Dunne helped Ireland register its first win of the campaign.

After the game, McCarthy expressed his satisfaction at

seeing two alternative names on the scoresheet – as opposed to the usual suspects Keane and Quinn – and challenged others such as Duff to follow suit.

'When somebody else other than Robbie Keane or Niall Quinn scores it is a bonus for us, because we need other people chipping in with goals rather than rely on the same ones,' McCarthy said.

'And, while we still need the likes of Kevin Kilbane and Damien Duff to embellish their contributions by chipping in with goals, it was mission accomplished.'

Although he'd become a peripheral figure within the Ireland setup, at least Damien Duff's starting place at Ewood Park was safe – or so he thought. After lining-up from the start of every Blackburn league game thus far that season, he returned to the northwest following the victory over Estonia with his sights set on helping Rovers put the brakes on Fulham's blistering start to the campaign. The boss, though, had other ideas.

Former France international midfielder Jean Tigana had made an immediate impact since taking the reins at Craven Cottage that summer, guiding Fulham to nine league wins out of nine ahead of Blackburn's visit that weekend.

Talking the day before the game, Tigana's counterpart Graeme Souness explained just why, in his opinion, the runaway leaders had enjoyed such success – and it didn't bode well for wide boy Damien Duff.

'They don't have any wingers,' Souness said. 'But they have ten outfield players who work their socks off. If you are going to be successful you need that. I don't think there is such a thing as wingers any more and they are proving that. The day of the winger is gone – that was a term from thirty years ago. You can't have people in your team who go out wide and wait for the ball. Fulham don't have wingers and their style works.'

If Souness's comment that the 'day of the winger is gone' didn't cause Duff too much concern – he wasn't just any old winger after all – then the manager's subsequent team selection certainly did.

Having seen his side slip towards mid-table after taking just a single point from their previous four games, Souness felt it was time for a shake-up. Duff was axed, and forced to take up a position on the bench that had become all too familiar at international level.

The player himself, of course, took it on the chin and waited for his next chance, which wasn't long in coming. The game at Fulham, which Rovers lost 2–1, was followed by another trip to London, this time a midweek clash with Wimbledon.

Duff was restored to the side and contributed to a vital 2–0 victory that sparked a much-needed run of six straight league wins for Blackburn. Not that Duff made any further contributions to that run. A hamstring injury kept him on the sidelines for more than five weeks, forcing him to miss out not only on Rovers' revival but also Ireland's 15 November friendly with Finland in Dublin.

He did return to the side in late November, though, and as 2000 drew to a close there were enough signs to suggest that 2001 might be a prosperous one for Duff. Blackburn were in the top three and Ireland – albeit with Duff playing a marginal role – were making decent headway in their World Cup qualifying group.

By the time Ireland resumed their World Cup campaign, with successive away trips to Cyprus and Andorra in March, things certainly were looking up for Duff. Blackburn had established the sort of winning consistency that had forced many bookmakers to install them as pre-season favourites for promotion, and Duff's impressive form had been a major factor in Rovers' drive towards the top of the table.

All that was missing from Duff's game was a goal. He hadn't found the target since netting twice in Blackburn's 6–1 Worthington Cup demolition of Rochdale back in September and hadn't scored in the league all season.

While the title would almost certainly end up in the hands off Tigana's Fulham, the race for the second automatic promotion spot was gathering pace. So Rovers' trip to face fellow promotion chasers Birmingham City on 14 March seemed like the perfect time for Duff to break his duck.

He duly obliged, and in some style, too. On an appalling pitch, he picked up possession a good distance from goal before accelerating his way through a trail of defenders and slipping the ball beneath Birmingham keeper Ian Bennett. It sealed a vital 2–0 win for the visitors that took them up to third place in the table, level on points with second-placed Bolton.

The manager was clearly satisfied with one winger whose day was certainly not gone. 'A wonderful football player who is starting to grasp what it's all about,' said Souness, whose team was undoubtedly the one in form.

Duff was just relieved to register his first league goal in almost a year, telling reporters, 'I've always been capable of that. I've been dribbling around players all season without hitting the back of the net. I've been shanking shots all over the place.'

His form had been so good, in fact, that both Sunderland and Bobby Robson's Newcastle were reportedly keen to offer him an immediate route back into the Premiership. A number of newspapers claimed that Newcastle were preparing to make a bid – most estimated in the region of £3–5 million, with some suggesting that Stephen Glass would be offered in part-exchange – after their director of football Gordon Milne reportedly watched Duff in Blackburn's 2–1 defeat away to Nottingham Forest in February.

Ironically, reports linking Duff to Sunderland reckoned that Peter Reid was interested in a straight swap deal with Kevin Kilbane, a player in direct competition with Duff for a place in the Ireland side. Kilbane, still a favourite of Ireland boss Mick McCarthy, had fallen out of favour at the Stadium of Light, and Reid, it was rumoured, was willing to do business.

With the speculation mounting, and talk of Newcastle's interest refusing to go away, Rovers moved quickly to put the record straight.

'Damien Duff is not for sale, end of story,' announced Graeme Souness. 'There's absolutely no chance I'd be prepared to let him go.'

Just in case his message hadn't quite filtered through to the chasing pack, the Blackburn boss reiterated his stance at the beginning of March. 'Damien's working extremely hard and he's getting the defensive part of his game together. He's quality, a top-drawer player who takes people on at pace. There's not a chance he will be sold.'

Ten days after his wonder strike at St Andrews, Duff was back on the World Cup trail with Ireland. Despite his dazzling club form he was still made to wait 82 minutes before entering the fray in a 4–0 beating of Cyprus, a game in which Roy Keane marked his fiftieth international appearance with a double strike.

But that elusive international starting spot would not be long in coming for the twenty-two-year-old Duff. The erratic form of his Ewood Park colleague Jason McAteer was becoming a topic of serious debate, with his place on the right-hand side of midfield seemingly under threat.

The press and public were not the only ones engaging in such a debate, it transpired, as Mick McCarthy himself decided it was finally time for a change. Four days after the defeat of Cyprus, Ireland would face international minnows Andorra in Barcelona with a rejuvenated Damien Duff operating – from the beginning – on the right wing.

It was the first time that Duff had taken his place in Ireland's starting line-up since a 1–0 Euro 2000 qualifying defeat away to Croatia in September 1999, some eighteen months earlier, and McCarthy's decision to include him was the subject of much interest among the media. It was just reward, they said, for a player who was clearly flourishing under Blackburn boss Graeme Souness.

It also brought into focus another factor that had helped Duff rediscover his best form – his weight. While never carrying the sort of 'timber' that saw the likes of Jan Molby and Mick Quinn become the inevitable targets of terrace taunts, Duff – by his own admission – had not always adhered to the strictest of diets. It was something the man himself was more than happy to talk about in the pre-match press conference.

'I feel a lot better now, even if I won the Player of the Season last year [at Blackburn] while being a fat old yolk,' he said.

'It's not like I'm a big drinker… I'm just a big eater. But I've cut down on the food and I'm eating a lot less now. In the past I used to get a lot of slagging from the lads because they knew I ate big mounds of food, and I found it very difficult not to pile on the weight.

'But I've worked hard to lose about a stone and I'm a better player for it, more confident both on and off the pitch, and Graeme Souness has got the best out of me since he became manager at Blackburn … You have to play well to stay in the side, he's ruthless like that.

'I definitely feel stronger and I think I'm a cleverer player as well. I'm delighted to be back. Playing for Ireland is the greatest thing ever and it is nice to get a chance to show what I can do.'

McCarthy was keen to explain the reasoning behind his decision by highlighting the progress that Duff had made in recent months. He told the press, 'He's a more confident, more thoughtful player. He's not just a bag of tricks any more, though he still has the skill and pace.

'He came in at the same time as Robbie [Keane], but it

has taken him a little longer. Nothing fazed Robbie and it was probably remiss of us to expect that Damien would adapt as easily.

'Damien is a different type of character, but he's now developing the way I always believed he would. He is a quality player.'

It seemed that all eyes were on the young Blackburn winger, including those of Ireland's World Cup heroes of the past. Former striker John Aldridge wrote in the *Mirror*, 'Damien Duff could be in line to play a big part, and it would be good to see him take his chance on the wing. He should have a great future for Ireland, and it's time to deliver as far as he's concerned.'

The match itself had a certain mystery surrounding its build-up after an anonymous tip-off that the Andorra squad included up to six ineligible players. A FIFA commissioner lined up the teams in their respective hotels and checked the passport of every player in a bizarre pre-match ritual.

With all suspicions firmly dispelled, Ireland, as expected, cantered to a 3–0 victory that took them to the top of the group (on goal difference) after Portugal could only draw 2–2 at home to Holland.

Duff was not among the scorers, as Ian Harte (from the penalty spot), Kevin Kilbane and Matt Holland all found the target to maintain Ireland's impressive momentum. He did, however, justify his place in the team by transferring the attacking prowess he'd been showing on a weekly basis at Blackburn onto the international stage. It was a performance that Duff's manager was more than happy with.

'He worked hard,' said McCarthy afterwards. 'It was difficult for him, because they worked so hard to stop him. But his dribbling skills were giving us momentum in the first half, which was something we had been lacking. I was pleased with him.'

Further praise came from the *Irish Times*, who claimed that 'Only Roy Keane and Damien Duff could be reckoned to have caused the opposition real problems on a consistent basis'; while Roy Curtis of the *Mirror* was among a growing band calling for Duff to be given a regular starting role. 'Duff's daring, his pace, his creative ingenuity terrifies defenders,' he wrote. 'The choice between him and Jason McAteer should be as easy to make as one between a week in the Seychelles or Skegness.'

Unfortunately for Duff, he was unable to consolidate his place in the side when Andorra came to Dublin the following month due to a troublesome hamstring. The problem flared up when leaders Fulham visited Ewood Park for a midweek top-of-the-table clash with second-placed Rovers on 11 April.

With a thirteen-point cushion at the summit, Fulham were destined for the title, and, even if they lost to their closest challengers, it would surely only delay the inevitable.

Rovers, meanwhile, desperately needed the points to maintain their own push for a top-flight return, and with the prized scalp of the champions elect on offer there was a tremendous buzz around Ewood Park on the evening of the match.

Graeme Souness had managed to stir things up even further before the game when he audaciously suggested that

Blackburn, and not the virtually unassailable leaders Fulham, were in his opinion 'the best footballing team in the division'.

It seemed he may have had a point when, after six minutes, Duff was involved in the move that saw Matt Jansen give Rovers the lead. It was to be Duff's last major contribution, though. Shortly after helping his side break the deadlock, he felt a familiar discomfort in his hamstring and, with just twelve minutes gone, he was replaced by Stig Inge Bjornebye.

From then onwards, things went from bad to worse for Souness. Despite seeing the visitors reduced to ten men after Rufus Brevett's dismissal, Fulham levelled on the stroke of half-time through Louis Saha and showed admirable resolve before mustering up a dramatic last-minute winner to leave them just one more win away from the Premiership.

Blackburn were still well set to achieve their own objective of going up (they were three points ahead of third-placed Bolton), but they faced the prospect of having to do so without one of their star performers. The injury to Duff, it was feared, may rule him out of Rovers' run-in as well as Ireland's World Cup qualifiers against Andorra (25 April), Portugal (2 June) and Estonia (6 June).

'If it's as bad as we fear, his season is over and that's another disappointment,' Souness admitted afterwards. 'In the second half they would have been really stretched if Damien had been out there. He was taking people on in that last third of the field and was a real danger. He may well have played his last game of the season. It's very disappointing and a real blow to us.'

So Duff could only watch as Rovers overcame the Fulham

blip and regained the sort of form that had seen them lose just once in nineteen league games before Tigana and his boys had performed their Ewood Park smash-and-grab raid.

There was, however, some good news for Rovers' crocked wing wonder. At the end of April he was named in the PFA Division One Team of the Year, the composition of which gave a clear indication of the section's two outstanding teams. With six Fulham players and four from Blackburn (Duff was joined by teammates Henning Berg, David Dunn and Matt Jansen) Birmingham left-back Martin Grainger was the only player to break the duopoly.

Even better news was to follow. Having recovered from his hamstring injury ahead of schedule, Duff discovered that his season was far from over. He would be fit for Ireland's World Cup double-header in June and, what was more, he would have a part to play in Blackburn's tense finale.

After amassing eighty-seven points from forty-four games, Rovers knew the brief was simple for them ahead of their penultimate game of the season away to Preston North End: win, and a Premiership place would be theirs. Providing the team with a timely boost was Duff, back in the side after a three-week absence.

A draw would have left Souness's side needing to get a result from a tricky-looking trip to Gillingham on the final day, and, after they'd spurned a series of chances at Deepdale, that seemed a likely scenario as the match entered its last twenty minutes goalless.

Rovers could always rely on Matt Jansen, though, and the striker was once again on the right spot in the seventy-second minute to nod home his twenty-third league goal of an excellent season to delight Blackburn's travelling army of supporters.

With no further goals, it was mission accomplished for Souness and his men. After two years outside the top tier, Blackburn were back in the big time, and Damien Duff was a Premiership player once again.

It was a fitting end to a campaign that had begun with Blackburn suffering the sad loss of the club's most influential figure of recent times, Jack Walker. Steel magnate Walker, who died of cancer at the age of seventy-one, invested millions of pounds in his local team and was rewarded with the 1994–5 Premiership title. One of his last wishes was that Rovers would make a swift return to the top flight, and Graeme Souness was happy to oblige.

'It's fitting that the season should end this way,' Souness said to the press afterwards. 'Jack was a wise old man. He knew it was going to be very hard but he must be a happy man looking down on us tonight. I just wish I was sharing a bottle of his best Bordeaux with him. He would have been proud of this team and what they have achieved and we all know what this club meant to him.

'My players deserve great credit. They got labelled fat cats last season, maybe deservedly so. But there's no way I can be critical of them this year.

'Every game we have played has been like a cup final for the opposing team because of the legacy of one man – Jack Walker.'

Ireland, without Duff (who, McCarthy confirmed, would definitely have started had he been fit), overcame the shock of falling behind to beat Andorra 3–1. They were in good shape as they approached the business end of their qualifying campaign, and they had to be, because next up was a game that was likely to have a crucial bearing on the outcome of a group from which they, Portugal and Holland still harboured serious hopes of progressing.

As it turned out, the visit of unbeaten Portugal to Lansdowne Road in June 2001 proved particularly significant for Duff. It was a match he would come to regard as the 'turning point' of his international career.

His injury-enforced inactivity saw him relegated once again to the bench, but Duff did enter the fray after sixty minutes. Although not seemingly significant at the time, his introduction – into a game that was drawn 1–1 following Roy Keane and Luis Figo's exchange of goals – would have a real bearing on Ireland's memorable World Cup adventure the following summer.

The significance was in the role that Duff was handed. Replacing the ineffective Robbie Keane with half an hour remaining and the game still goalless, he was told to attack the Portuguese defence through the middle as opposed to his usual position on the wing.

The role was not completely alien to Duff – he had operated there for Blackburn – and the impact he made was remarkable, immediately causing the visitors problems with his darting runs and sparkling invention. It was a performance applauded by a host of the following day's newspapers. The *Irish Times* said: 'Duff sparkled, twisted and turned, and was punished by heavy challenges. Suddenly, Ireland were a threat – and not to themselves.'

It wasn't just members of the press who were queuing up to lavish praise on a player fresh from helping Blackburn end their two-year Premiership exile. Speaking to the *Sun*, Ireland teammate Gary Breen was equally impressed – though not surprised – by Duff's supersub showing. 'Damien has got the ability to walk around people. He will take the Premiership by storm next season,' he said.

'He was fantastic against Portugal but I wasn't surprised as he had been brilliant all week in training. He lulls defenders into a false sense of security by the way he walks around in a hunched style. He looks knackered and then suddenly he is away from you.'

Kevin Kilbane was also full of admiration: 'I thought Damien was sharp and lively when he came on. He caused them a considerable amount of trouble and his introduction was probably the turning point in the game for us. He was excellent but we all know what he is capable of.'

Most importantly of all, Mick McCarthy was another to voice his approval: 'Duffer had an amazing impact when he came on. Whether he can have that same impact from the start remains to be seen, but he was very effective against Portugal. He certainly put a marker down for himself.'

For McCarthy, it had been an eventful afternoon. A match that was given an extra edge during its build-up due to key defender Fernando Couto's sudden FIFA-induced ban due to alleged drug use and Ian Harte's public accusation that Figo went to ground a little too easily, ended with the Ireland manager embroiled in a heated touchline exchange after his Portuguese counterpart Antonio Oliveira refused his offer of a handshake.

But, once the dust had settled, McCarthy was able to reflect on another fine result for his unbeaten side. It also left the boss in no doubt as to what was required for Ireland to achieve their ultimate goal of World Cup qualification. He declared that Ireland must win their remaining three games in order to qualify because, he predicted, Portugal (who were three points behind with a game in hand) would take maximum points from their final four games. With Cyprus (twice), Estonia and Andorra providing the opposition, it was difficult to disagree.

Exciting times for the Irish then, and certainly for Damien Duff. Despite McCarthy's reservations about his ability to influence a game from the start, the excellent manner in which Duff had adapted to a central attacking role against Portugal gave him a great chance of starting the match away to Estonia four days later.

Also in Duff's favour was the fact that Robbie Keane, who until recently had been an automatic selection in one of the two striking roles, was clearly out of sorts. Keane had not found the target at international level since he opened Ireland's World Cup qualifying account in the 2–2 draw away to Holland nine months earlier, while an ankle injury and a limited number of starts for his new club Leeds United meant that Ireland's brightest young striker was struggling to find his best form.

So it was with some confidence that Duff looked ahead to the Estonia trip. Speaking to the *Sun*, he said, 'Obviously, I want to start. I always do. I was buzzing to get on against Portugal but I want to play the full 90 minutes, not just bits here and there.

'Mick has tried me in a few positions now, but he hasn't really tied me down to one role in particular. He has questioned whether I could have the same impact over the full 90 minutes. But why not? If he gives me the chance I'll show him.'

Duff was optimistic not only of his own chances of playing a bigger part for his country but also of Ireland's odds of making it to Japan & South Korea – hopefully without running the risk of suffering further play-off agony: 'People say Portugal are in the driving seat now, but I disagree. We are still in control of our own destiny. We will finish with the same number of points if we both win all our remaining games. It couldn't be tighter.

Another issue on which Duff was quizzed was the absence of the suspended Roy Keane, about which he added, 'Roy is one of the best players in the world, isn't he? He hadn't played in six weeks and still bossed the game against Portugal. He's just world class. Obviously we're going to miss him, but we've got a lot of experienced players who are all leaders.'

So Duff was impressed with the way his manager was working. He was even more impressed, no doubt, when the team to face Estonia was announced. As predicted, McCarthy felt it was time to take Robbie Keane out of the firing line and instead employ Duff as Niall Quinn's strike partner.

A 2–0 win for Ireland meant that McCarthy and his men could rest easy over the summer, safe in the knowledge that their destiny was still in their own control. The other Keane's replacement, Matt Holland, once again demonstrated a useful knack of scoring important goals by adding to Richard Dunne's opening strike in Tallinn and clinching another vital victory that kept Ireland in pole position.

GROUP 2 TABLE AT 7 JUNE 2001						
	P	W	D	L	Pts	GD
Rep. of Ireland	8	5	3	0	18	+13
Portugal	7	4	3	0	15	+13
Holland	7	4	2	1	14	+13
Estonia	7	2	1	4	7	−6
Cyprus	7	2	1	4	7	−12
Andorra	8	0	0	8	0	−21

The question of whether or not Duff could be as effective from the start of a match as when he's introduced late on, when his pace causes tiring defences no end of problems, seemed to be answered in *The Times*'s assessment of his performance: 'Duff twisted his markers every which way and although he did not contribute directly to the goals, the Estonia defenders were in such a state of panic that they barely knew the time of day.'

It was a fitting end to an excellent season for Duff. Having played a key role in Blackburn's triumphant push for a Premiership return, he was also making good progress at international level. A campaign that had started with Duff on the fringes of the Ireland squad finished with the Ballyboden boy establishing himself as a key part of Mick McCarthy's World Cup plans.

Not that anyone had ever doubted his ability – or his potential future as an international star – since he burst onto the Premiership scene as a raw eighteen-year-old. But, after he had dropped out of the top flight with Blackburn and lost his way under Ewood Park boss Brian Kidd, his form inevitably dipped.

It probably hadn't helped matters that the rising fortunes of Ireland's other young starlet Robbie Keane had – until recently – shown no signs of letting up, as the Tallaght-born striker clinched a dream move to Serie A giants Inter Milan after making a stunning impact on the Premiership with Coventry City.

Duff, though, was back. He was now delivering the sort of dazzling performances that his unquestionable talent had always promised, and he started the 2001–2 season exactly as he'd ended the previous one.

With the crunch September visit of Holland to Dublin less than three weeks away, Ireland drew 2–2 with Croatia in a friendly at Lansdowne Road. It was there, in his twenty-first international appearance, that Duff claimed his first senior goal for his country as he was once again employed in a central attacking role – this time alongside Keane.

It wasn't just his goal – an excellent angled drive into the top corner – that drew the plaudits in the following day's papers. His all-round showing caught the eye as he cranked up the pressure on Mick McCarthy to hand him a starting role against the Dutch. The *Irish Times* wrote: 'The one thing that did emerge as a positive for Ireland was the performance of Damien Duff up front. He was sharp, moved into spaces well and took his goal very clinically. He also blended well with Robbie Keane – whose sharpness was heartening – and now, with Niall Quinn not ruled out, McCarthy has a potentially pleasant dilemma up front. Over the past five games, Duff has emerged as arguably our best player (the boy Roy aside) and should start against Holland.'

The Sun simply said: 'Duff's goal was worth the admission price alone.' And *The Times* opined, 'If and when Niall Quinn is fit, he might find that his guaranteed place in the side has disappeared.'

Duff, of course, was typically modest when reflecting on his first goal for Ireland. 'I was just happy to finally get my name on the scoresheet,' he said. 'It was a great buzz, scoring at Lansdowne Road. But, if I'm honest, it was about time I got a goal.'

The excellent performance of his new-look front two gave McCarthy plenty to think about ahead of the Holland clash. Should he stick with his favoured little-and-large combo of big Niall Quinn plus one other, or should he go for broke and frighten the Dutch with a pair of pacey tricksters?

It was a dilemma he was prepared to mull over in public. He denied claims that Ireland were one-dimensional with Niall Quinn in the team, and suggested that his side's favoured approach was to play the ball into feet regardless of whom he selected in the striking positions. He also spoke of his delight at seeing Duff and Keane cause Croatia so many problems at Lansdowne Road. Big Niall's huge presence had always made him difficult for opponents to handle, but the pace, movement and balance of Duff and Keane presented defenders with an entirely different challenge altogether.

McCarthy was particularly pleased with the way that Duff had sparkled in a central role. In the wake of the Croatia game he told the *Sun*, 'Duffer is so direct and elusive. He could play up front in the Premiership, but that's Graeme Souness's call, not mine. He goes left when you expect him to go right and vice versa. He can dribble and wriggle his way around defenders as well. Is there anything he can't do?

'But he's so quick, defenders can't get near him and, nowadays, you don't get kicked as much from behind. Defenders go to nick the ball off him and he's gone in a flash.'

McCarthy also felt that Duff's successful adaptation to a striking role would help Robbie Keane end his barren run at international level. He added, 'Robbie, in fairness, is a great kid. I'm not saying he needs a kick up the backside, but it can be a very humbling experience when somebody else comes into your position and steals your thunder. But it might not do him any harm.'

One man who'd been keeping a keen eye on Duff's international progress was Graeme Souness – and he liked what he saw. He'd been impressed by the outstanding manner in which Duff had been operating for the national team and knew that the form of his left-winger would be a key factor in Blackburn's attempt to re-establish themselves as a Premiership force.

Speaking to the *Sun*, Souness challenged the young Rover to replicate his international form in the blue and white of Blackburn: 'I want Damien to emulate his international form in his performances for Rovers this season. For someone like Damien, who has flirted with the Premier League before, this is a very big season for him.

'He's one of several youngsters we have who have played in the top flight but not on a regular basis. So he will want to prove and establish himself as a main player in the Premier League and I believe he certainly has the ability to do that.

'He's got something which is rare in the game. He's someone who can take people on and dribble past them with pace. And the encouraging thing for me is he's currently the fittest he's probably ever been since he's been at this club.

'So the stage is set for him to become a real star this season – if he wants to.'

Duff's response was as swift as one of his lightning bursts beyond an opposing full-back. One week before Ireland's meeting with Holland he warmed up by scoring a fine goal in Blackburn's 2–1 win against Tottenham – their first Premiership win of the season after losing at Derby and then drawing with Manchester United.

Receiving the ball out on the left-hand side somewhere near the halfway line, Duff sliced his way through the Spurs defence before firing beyond goalkeeper Neil Sullivan with his lesser-favoured right foot. It proved to be the winner and, inevitably, the question of Duff's worth to the Rovers side was once again raised after the match. Souness was happy to answer.

'We know Damien's capable of doing that and we expect Damien to continue this form he's shown since pre-season,' he said. 'If you know Damien you'll know that he wants to do well and I think this is his year to do well. If he can avoid injuries he'll show people he's a top talent in this league.'

Back in the Premiership and with glowing praise from his bosses of both club and country ringing in his ears, Duff had every right to be bursting with confidence as he headed off to face the Dutch in Dublin.

With McCarthy unable to hide his admiration for his winger-turned-striker, it seemed that Duff, who for so long had been competing with the likes of Mark Kennedy, Kevin Kilbane and Jason McAteer for a place out wide, was now a certain starter at centre-forward. The question now was, who would start alongside him?

One of his possible sidekicks, Niall Quinn, certainly didn't begrudge the youngster his moment in the spotlight. 'In fairness, Duffer's flying,' Quinn told the Press Association. 'He's on top of his form right now and picks himself. At this moment he could not be playing any better. He's going to pose a huge threat to the Dutch. Hopefully they won't know what's hit them.'

Another man attracting a lot of attention as the game approached was Jaap Stam, with the football world still reeling from the Dutch defender's sudden exit from Old Trafford. He departed under a cloud, heading to Lazio for a fee in the region of £16.5 million. Mick McCarthy was confident that Ireland, and Duff in particular, were ready to give the big centre-half another major headache. McCarthy, who admitted there would be calls for his head if Ireland were to lose, told the press, 'I know if I was Jaap Stam I wouldn't be relishing the prospect of facing Damien Duff. I can't speak for Jaap Stam, but I can speak from my own personal experience as a former central defender. And if I was Jaap Stam, I would be concerned. Very concerned indeed.

'A big central defender is always happier marking a big frontman because you know what to expect. But small, pacey players like Duffer are a different proposition entirely. They're a damn nuisance. They run about your feet, peel off your shoulder and twist and turn. They can give you the runaround if you're not careful.

'Duffer offers us something down the middle that we haven't had before… he's muddied the waters slightly. Quinny's been there all the time, but Duffer has put down a real marker for himself with his performances up front.'

Stam himself was well aware of the potential danger posed by Duff, telling the *Sun*: 'It doesn't matter who plays, it will still be difficult. Robbie Keane has a big reputation but Damien Duff is also a good player. I have played against him once, maybe twice, and I have seen him in action for Blackburn a lot on television. He has impressed me. He is very skilful and dangerous. It won't be any easier for me against him.'

Duff, meanwhile, made sure that Holland were fully aware of the challenge ahead. Ireland had not lost a competitive match in Dublin since Austria won 3–1 in a Euro '96 qualifier more than six years earlier. It was a record of which Duff was proud to remind everyone.

'Teams always find Dublin a very, very difficult place to come to,' he told the press. 'We've done very well here over the past number of years so we're all looking forward to playing Holland. We have nothing to fear.

'I don't even know if I'm playing yet. I will just have to wait and see what Mick's decided to do when he names the team.'

What followed was an unforgettable afternoon for Irish fans, another addition to a memorable collection of classic encounters that have illuminated the recent history of Irish football.

'The game against Holland was the one that gave us the belief,' remembers Niall Quinn in his autobiography.

It's not difficult to see why. After Holland had dominated for long spells while failing to take their chances, Gary Kelly was sent-off just twelve minutes into the second half when he was shown a second yellow card for a challenge on Marc Overmars. Undermanned but certainly not undeterred, Ireland showed remarkable spirit to go on and win the game 1–0.

The scorer of the only goal was Jason McAteer, who converted Steve Finnan's sixty-seventh-minute cross to settle the outcome and leave Ireland assured of at least a play-off place. According to the *Sunday Times*, the role of Duff (who started in attack alongside Robbie Keane) in the goal should not be understated: '[The cross] fell towards Stam, but instead of clearing, he froze, paralysed by Duff, the pesky whippet, who darted across his bows.'

It was a sweet victory for Ireland. For Holland, who had broken Irish hearts at the 1988 European Championships, the 1994 World Cup and in a Euro '96 play-off, their chances of appearing at the 2002 World Cup finals had now virtually vanished.

Duff again repaid his manager's faith in him with a

performance that had newspaper reporters purring. The *Sunday Telegraph* talked of a 'supremely confident Duff' and said that 'the Irish eventually found relief in Duff's inspirational running. The Blackburn player seems to have come of age on the international scene.'

The *Sunday Times*, meanwhile, commented on Duff's 'remarkable progress' and claimed, 'Damien Duff simply grew stronger when he had to soldier alone up front for most of the last 20 minutes. If he can be restored to his best position wide on the left, or for next best on the right, Duff can be a tremendous asset for the next decade.'

McCarthy, who claimed it was his best ever victory, later admitted that his decision to use Duff as a central attacker against Holland was made during a trip to Old Trafford, when he went to watch Fulham defender Steve Finnan play against Manchester United but couldn't help but notice an interesting confrontation taking place elsewhere.

'I noticed how Louis Saha's pace destroyed Jaap Stam,' he said. 'I knew then that when we played Holland I would put Damien Duff in the middle to run at Stam. It worked a treat. Even when we were down to ten men he was still giving the Dutch hell. Duffer was brilliant in that role.'

The celebrations lasted long into the night but Duff, one of the chief architects of the famous victory, couldn't be found getting merry in any of Dublin's nightspots. For him, the post-match routine involved a short trip home to Ballyboden and a quiet night in with brother Jamie, watching England beat Germany 5–1 on TV.

'That came out when I was asked in a press conference

what I'd done on the evening of our great win,' he has since said. 'I said I went home and watched the England game with me little brother. They laughed at me as if it was something bad. I like my night out, but I don't get to see my little brother that often. So I stayed in with him. Grand.'

Despite their brilliant win against Holland, and despite the fact that they were still unbeaten, Ireland were still likely to finish second in the group because Portugal's 7–1 hammering of Andorra had significantly boosted their goal difference and left Ireland facing the likelihood of another place in the play-offs.

As their final qualifier approached, the only way that Ireland could secure automatic qualification was by getting a result against Cyprus in Dublin and hoping that Estonia could spring a surprise in Portugal. That didn't happen of course, as Portugal ran out 5–0 winners to render Ireland's 4–0 drubbing of Cyprus pretty much meaningless, although not for Niall Quinn.

The Sunderland striker celebrated his thirty-fifth birthday by scoring a record twenty-first goal for his country, taking him one clear of previous record holder Frank Stapleton.

Missing for Ireland was Duff, who had sustained another hamstring problem two weeks prior to the match, during Blackburn's 1–0 Premiership win against Everton. The team managed perfectly well without him, though, and the picture was now crystal clear – beat Iran in a two-legged play-off and Ireland were off to the Far East.

The only problem was that Ireland weren't very good at

FINAL GROUP 2 TABLE						
	P	W	D	L	Pts	GD
Portugal	10	7	3	0	24	+26
Rep. of Ireland	10	7	3	0	24	+18
Holland	10	6	2	2	20	+21
Estonia	10	2	2	6	8	–16
Cyprus	10	2	2	6	8	–18
Andorra	10	0	0	10	0	–31

play-offs. Their last three attempts at qualifying for major tournaments had ended at that very same stage. First, in a one-off match at Anfield in December 1995, a goal in each half from Patrick Kluivert was enough to secure Holland a 2–0 win and a spot at Euro '96. A 3–2 aggregate defeat against Belgium then cost Ireland a place at the 1998 World Cup, while arguably the most excruciating defeat of all came when Turkey sneaked through to the finals of Euro 2000 on away goals following an ill-tempered affair in which Duff appeared from the bench in both legs.

He didn't appear in either leg of the November 2001 play-off with Iran, however. Having failed to overcome the hamstring injury that forced him out of the previous month's clash with Cyprus, Duff adopted the role of anxious onlooker, unable to influence what would have been the two biggest games of his career thus far.

In fact, they probably were still the biggest games of his career, even though he was to play no active part in them. If Ireland won, Duff would have the chance to grace the greatest stage of all, emulating his heroes of Italia '90 and

USA '94.

His teammates took a huge step towards qualification by winning the first leg 2–0 at Lansdowne Road, with Ian Harte bagging a penalty and Robbie Keane demonstrating expert timing to end his fourteen-month international goal drought and give his side a two-goal cushion to take into the away leg.

For the return in Tehran five days later, Ireland would have to do without their inspirational skipper Roy Keane (whose knee injury had flared up after the first leg), while Niall Quinn's problematic back meant that he was another nonstarter.

There were plenty of other players willing to assume the role of play-off hero, though, and, after Shay Given made a number of excellent saves to add to the couple he pulled off towards the end of the first match, Ireland battled through.

A last-minute goal may have meant a 1–0 defeat and the end of a sixteen-match unbeaten run but Ireland, 2–1 aggregate winners, couldn't care less. Their play-off hoodoo had been well and truly smashed.

Mick McCarthy, understandably, made no effort to mask his joy in his post-match address: 'I'm delighted for me, my players, my staff, the supporters and my family because they won't have to witness a grumpy dad coming home again. It's so difficult to articulate how I feel but I'm immensely proud. When the whistle went, it was a wonderful, wonderful feeling.

'Make no mistake, we deserved it. I believe real heroes are people who fight in wars and die for their country, but in football terms they are all heroes for me.'

Unfortunately for Duff, his injury-enforced absence meant

that he missed out on the celebrations in Iran. His time would come, though, and in a way that would change his life. Ireland were off to the World Cup finals, and, although he may not have realised it at the time, Damien Duff was on the brink of international superstardom.

CHAPTER 6

Survival Instincts

'Most bosses going to Japan and
Korea would love to have Duffer in their side.'
ALAN KELLY, JANUARY 2002

The greatest show on earth was little more than six
months away, and Ireland would once again be playing
a part. But who would assume the starring role? Could any
of Mick McCarthy's young guns revel in the company of the
world's leading players and elevate themselves to superhero
status? Their expectant green army of supporters held its
collective breath.

For now, though, thoughts of rubbing shoulders with
Ronaldo, Batistuta, Del Piero, Raul and Zidane would have
to wait. Damien Duff had other things on his mind.
Primarily, his objective was to help Blackburn Rovers retain
its standing as a Premiership club, a position he and his
Ewood Park colleagues had fought so hard to attain
throughout the previous season.

When Duff returned to action following a lay-off of almost

two months, for a home match with Liverpool on 17 November, Blackburn could hardly be considered relegation contenders. Graeme Souness's side occupied a healthy eighth place in the Premiership after claiming seventeen points from their opening twelve games, with a 7–1 thumping of West Ham the highlight of the season so far.

Souness, though, had been around long enough to know that no team had ever secured its top-flight status by November. And, with the impressive early-season form of a newly promoted team so often fuelled by the momentum created by their recent elevation, there's always a danger that the honeymoon period can end – sometimes in alarmingly abrupt fashion – at any time. For Rovers, this proved to be the case.

The talk surrounding that first game back for Duff was not of relegation, but of the Blackburn left-winger's inclusion. With the game coming just two days after the second leg of Ireland's World Cup play-off with Iran – a match that Duff withdrew from due to injury – Souness's decision to name Duff in his starting line-up was alleged to have caused something of a stir within the Irish camp.

The *Sunday Mirror* reported that a senior FAI official said, 'There was never a problem in getting Blackburn's Ireland players released for international games in the past – but there certainly is now.'

A diplomatic McCarthy, on the other hand, was keen to play down talk of a dispute. 'I depend on the goodwill of club managers for the release of players – for friendly games in particular – and I'm not about to go putting that relationship at risk,' he said.

'Duff has been carrying this injury for the better part of three months and I've no doubt that, if he'd been fit, he would have been released. Fortunately, we were able to qualify without him. But we definitely need him on board for the World Cup finals.'

The issue was subsequently put to bed – although it wouldn't be the last time the use of Duff would cause friction between his two managers.

Rovers drew with Liverpool and took just a single point from their next two games, against Chelsea and Middlesbrough, but if Souness was beginning to feel the first pangs of concern he certainly wasn't showing it. He seemed satisfied with the way his team were performing, and was particularly pleased with a player who had readjusted to life in the Premiership quite effortlessly – Damien Duff. It was as if he'd never been away.

'We feel that Damien has the potential to be a top, top man in the Premier League and we expect him to do that in the coming years,' Souness told the press, on the eve of his side's cross-Pennines clash with Leeds United.

'This year he has been held back a wee bit by his injury. But I think the respect teams show Damien is obvious to see because he's never just confronted by a full-back: he's confronted by a full-back and a covering defender or midfield player. People queue up against him because they know he can take you on, get to the by-line and cause all sorts of problems.'

Following a 2–1 league reverse at home to Leeds, Blackburn turned their attention to something that had become all too rare for Rovers fans in recent times – an extended cup run. Despite claiming the Premiership title in 1995 the club had not featured in a major cup final since 1960, and had not emerged victorious from such an occasion since Harry Healless lifted the FA Cup following a 3–1 win against Huddersfield Town in 1928.

There was a Full Members' Cup final victory over Charlton in 1987, but even the 25,000 Rovers die-hards who followed the club to Wembley that day knew that it didn't really count. With the best part of 75 years having passed since their last major triumph – and with almost every living Rovers supporter unable to recall it – another cup success was long overdue.

So, after disposing of Oldham, Middlesbrough and Manchester City in the early rounds, Blackburn fans looked forward to the Worthington Cup quarter-final visit of Arsenal with some relish.

The prestige of the League Cup (Worthington became its sponsor in 1998) had been tarnished in recent seasons as the Premiership's big guns fixed their sights elsewhere – namely on the game's most prestigious prize, the Champions League – and showed little interest in winning the competition, using it instead to field a mixture of fringe players and youth-team graduates whose first-team opportunities were otherwise limited.

Arsenal were one of those clubs, and boss Arsène Wenger did little to buck the trend when he took his team to Blackburn, making nine changes from the Gunners side who had secured a 3–2 Premiership win against Aston Villa in their previous outing. The manager, quite clearly, was finding it hard to get excited about the match, and once the game started it soon became evident that his players were, too.

With twenty-two minutes gone, Arsenal found themselves 3–0 down and on their way out, having been unable to deal with a blistering start by the home side. The chief tormentor was Duff, who set up Matt Jansen for his hat-trick strike, hit a post himself and had a hand in two other goals as Blackburn eventually won 4–0.

Regardless of the manner in which their opponents approached the contest, it was a comfortable, morale-boosting win for Blackburn that took them into the last four of what was still a major competition despite Arsène Wenger's protestations. In a move that further illustrated his disregard for the competition, Wenger questioned the convention of rewarding the cup winners with a place in Europe.

'The advantage of this competition is the European place, but I would give one more place to the championship,' he told the press pack. 'I feel it is more difficult to finish fifth or sixth in the Premiership.'

Souness refused to get carried away by the victory, choosing instead to remind everyone that the priority for him and his players was not cup glory but retaining the club's Premiership status.

He did, however, find time to reflect favourably on his spell in charge at Ewood Park, revealing his enjoyment at dealing with an exciting crop of youngsters that included Duff and two English players who were being tipped by some to force their way into Sven-Göran Eriksson's World Cup plans, Matt Jansen and David Dunn. Speaking to the *Sunday Express*, Souness said, 'There's nothing worse, and it's happened to me a couple of times at other clubs, when you finish training and you think "Have I made any impression today? Have I made a difference in a player's attitude? Have they learned anything?"

'You feel as if you might as well have spoken to a concrete post or to the cow in the next field. But here at Blackburn, because they are so young, they want to learn. I am under no illusions they might well change as they get older. They might start to think they have all the answers. But I am very happy here.'

When Blackburn travelled to Charlton three days before Christmas on the back of three straight defeats Souness needed his young guns to deliver. Two of them – the 'Double-D Men' Duff and Dunn – duly did, each scoring after the break to ease temporarily any fears of a slump.

For Blackburn fans who made the trip to South London it was another chance to see Duff operate as a striker, a role that he had taken to so impressively at international level. The manager's decision to move his left-winger into a more advanced position, playing off the Italian Corrado Grabbi, was influenced by a problem that, Souness felt, was at the root of Rovers' problems: a lack of firepower.

It wasn't that Blackburn didn't have any strikers, even though front men Nathan Blake and Marcus Bent had both been offloaded since the start of the campaign. But, while Grabbi was struggling to justify the significant transfer fee Blackburn had parted with to sign him in the close season, Jansen – despite his Worthington Cup exploits – had failed to match his strike rate of the previous term, Mark Hughes was past his best at thirty-eight years of age and Egil Ostenstad was merely on the fringes.

So Souness made no secret of the fact that he was trying to strengthen his strike force, admitting that one of the players he was tracking was Parma's ex-Aston Villa centre forward Savo Milosevic.

In the meantime, he had to make do with what he'd got and, luckily for Souness, that included an in-form Duff. His goal, a neat finish with his right foot, and all-round display meant that his boss could approach the festive period in good spirit.

'Today we finished clinically, which is something we have not been doing lately,' Souness told reporters afterwards. 'We've played far better in the last three games and lost because we didn't have the finishing touch. We did today and it's made the difference.

'I thought Damien played very well today. It's not his position, although he has played there a few times for Ireland. But he's such a good finisher we can use him anywhere in the front line. He finished with his right foot, which is a collector's item.'

At the same time, Souness stressed that Duff still had some work to do before he could consider himself the finished article. Although he'd played well as a striker against Charlton, Duff's natural place was still considered to be out on the flank, from where his manager wanted to get more out of him and fellow wide boy Keith Gillespie.

Souness continued, 'I think [Gillespie and Duff] have been one of the pluses in recent weeks. Wide players – they no longer call themselves wingers – are a rarity these days and punters like people who can dribble the ball and can take players on with pace. We've got two of them and, when they are on song, we're very good to watch.

'But it's not just about being a forward-thinking player. They have to do their bit coming back and tucking in and be a midfield player when we've not got the ball. That's something they both have to improve on, but we're happy with their form.'

If Blackburn thought they'd cracked it after that win at the Valley, they were sadly mistaken. Three more defeats, all without scoring, made sure of that. And, although they proved that their win at Charlton was no fluke by completing the double over Alan Curbishley's men with a 4–1 thrashing at Ewood Park, the honeymoon period for the Premiership new-boys was definitely over.

In the wake of that 4–1 win *The Times* singled out Duff for special praise, saying: 'Damien Duff's *raison d'être* may once have been to bamboozle defenders before infuriating his manager with an eccentric final pass, but here his lateral thinking obeyed the wishes of his team. One 40-yard diagonal run, worthy of Alberto Tomba, the slalom legend, ended with a shot just inches wide.'

One of the Blackburn goalscorers against Charlton was a new signing who would play a key role in the club's fight for survival, even though his goals – of which there were many – had, until that point, more often affected events at the other end of the table.

When Graeme Souness began his search for a player with

the predatory instincts to capitalise on the many chances his side were creating, he was unlikely to find any more predatory than Andy Cole, a player who has had his critics (namely former England manager Glenn Hoddle, who questioned the striker's goals-to-chances ratio), but whose standing as one of the Premiership era's most prolific goalscorers is indisputable.

A Champions League and five-times Premiership winner with Manchester United, thirty-year-old Cole offered a wealth of experience and a proven goal touch in return for a fee somewhere in the region of £7.5 million. The man himself couldn't wait to get started.

'I never got the opportunity to play with Keith [Gillespie] at either Newcastle or Manchester United but I'm looking forward to getting on the end of his crosses,' he told the *People*. 'I know from watching him and Damien Duff that they both create a lot of chances.'

Thankfully for Cole those chances continued to materialise, and thankfully for Blackburn their new striker developed a handy knack of converting them. The cloud that was forming over the club's Premiership campaign was about to get a silver lining.

Damien Duff was in pretty good shape as the World Cup year of 2002 dawned. Although his team were occupying a position in the bottom half of the Premiership table, the enterprising vigour of their star winger cum occasional striker had been a refreshing feature of Blackburn Rovers' campaign.

League title contenders they were not, but they still had one eye on domestic glory. The draw for the Worthington Cup semi-finals had been kind to Rovers as they avoided their Premiership rivals Tottenham Hotspur and Chelsea and were paired with Sheffield Wednesday, a side whose sudden fall from grace had left them struggling near the foot of the First Division.

Blackburn showed little sympathy, though, as they took full advantage of their opponents' plight by securing a 2–1 advantage at the halfway stage of the tie after Craig Hignett and Andy Cole had both profited from Duff's first-half crosses at Hillsborough.

'Two great balls in from Damo,' was how Hignett described the service.

While Duff was far from satisfied with the display – 'We could have played a lot better but I'm pleased with the result' was his post-match assessment – others were not so reserved when evaluating the star man's performance.

The *Irish Times*, for instance, reckoned that, '[Duff's] form this season has elevated him behind only Ryan Giggs as the finest left-sided player in English football.' His form, inevitably, had not gone unnoticed elsewhere, and reports again linking him with a move to Liverpool marked the beginning of a huge new wave of transfer speculation.

Another inevitability, it seemed, was that Blackburn would reach their first major domestic cup final for forty-two years as the second leg of their semi-final with Sheffield Wednesday approached. And so it proved, with Duff scoring one and setting up another for Cole as Rovers won a highly entertaining game 4–2 to complete a 6–3 aggregate triumph.

It was a result that delighted the ecstatic home contingent among an Ewood Park crowd of almost 27,000. But, as Duff later revealed to the *Independent*, that mood hadn't quite been replicated by the victorious players.

'I wouldn't say the lads were really going mad in the dressing room,' he said. 'The league is the most important thing; this is just a big bonus.'

Whether that was actually the case or just the words of a man well versed in traditional football-speak we can't be sure. What was for certain was Duff's pleasure at seeing goal king Cole once again make the most of his meticulous approach work.

'I have been putting those sorts of ball in all season and have been waiting for someone to get on the end of them,' he added. 'I knew [when I crossed] that Andy would be there.'

In keeping with the pattern of his season thus far, the following weeks were laced with mixed fortunes for Duff. The second weekend in February saw Blackburn lose 2–0 away to Fulham, their tenth defeat in twelve Premiership games and a result that saw them slip into the bottom three. They still had the Worthington Cup final to look forward to, of course, but it was a match they would go into out of form and with the threat of relegation looming large.

The pain of sliding into the drop zone was eased just twenty-four hours later, when Duff edged out fellow contenders Ian Harte and Richard Dunne to land the Irish Young Player of the Year award.

It was typical of the recognition that Duff was now

receiving and, as the summer approached, the forthcoming World Cup was inevitably an increasingly popular topic of discussion. Ireland, it was being whispered, might just possess something of a secret weapon in the form of their dazzling Irish Rover.

Goalkeeper Alan Kelly, a teammate of Duff's at club and international level, certainly thought so. 'Damien's an exceptional player, and he's on fire at the moment,' Kelly told the *News of the World*. 'When he's on the ball, he can produce magical moments of inspiration. Most bosses going to Japan and Korea would love to have Duffer in their side.'

Two bosses did have him in their side, and both were extremely grateful. Graeme Souness, also in the *News of the World*, said, 'Damien's always been a bit special. People were talking about him when I arrived at Blackburn, and he really came into his own as an international last season. He has some very exciting skills, and with his fitness no longer in doubt, I think he has a big year ahead of him.'

McCarthy was just pleased that Duff had finally found his feet at international level, even if it had taken a little longer than some people had first predicted. For a long time he had battled it out with Kevin Kilbane, Mark Kennedy and Keith O'Neill for one of the most keenly contested spots in the Irish team – the left-wing position – but, after he had adapted to a series of roles at the highest level, Duff's prospects had improved markedly.

Now, with a player at his disposal who had proved himself to be equally dangerous on either flank or through the middle, McCarthy knew he had a devastating ace up his sleeve.

'I don't think anyone ever doubted Damien's ability,' McCarthy said. 'I believe he has all the qualities which go to make an exciting forward – good movement on and off the ball, lots of skill and a temperament that ensures he's never fazed by the big occasion. Put it all together and you have an exciting package. I'm grateful for the selection option he gives me.'

Three days after Duff was awarded his new title, Irish fans were given a chance to monitor the progress of their Young Player of the Year when Ireland played Russia in a friendly at Lansdowne Road.

Mick McCarthy was understandably excited at the prospect of developing the Duff–Keane strike partnership, so started the pair together in an experimental team that included the untried midfielders Steven Reid and Colin Healy.

It turned out to be a useful exercise for McCarthy, as Reid opened the scoring before Robbie Keane found the target to seal a 2–0 victory, with Healy emerging as one of the night's most impressive performers.

'It's going well,' said Duff, when quizzed about his striking alliance with Keane after the game. 'I've known Robbie for a good few years now and we've played together at underage level, so I understand how he plays and I thought we linked up well tonight.'

Duff was withdrawn at half-time as McCarthy's desire to get as extensive a look at his squad as possible resulted in a total of twelve substitutions. Even though he featured for only forty-five minutes, Duff showed enough flashes of brilliance to suitably excite those in attendance.

The Times claimed, 'Damien Duff displayed his full range of tricks in a series of electrifying bursts. The Russians had little idea how to stop him.' The *Sunday Times* suggested that Duff was 'quickly becoming the team's most important component after the captain [Roy Keane]... Duff's attitude and appetite are faultless.'

Former Ireland defender Mark Lawrenson was another pledging his allegiance to the Damien Duff fan club. He identified Duff as the man to give Ireland a spark of 'spontaneity' at the World Cup with his 'different and unpredictable' approach. Lawrenson wrote in the *Irish Times*: 'The player who really took my fancy was Damien Duff. Given the problems we have in moulding a productive striking partnership, Duff's form was most encouraging. He showed wonderful skill at coming off defenders. Duff and Robbie Keane have emerged as our best striking option and the Blackburn player holds the key for the way in which he can spin, run at defenders and really beat them.'

As Ireland's new-look strike force continued to flourish, one player who could have been forgiven for lamenting its emergence was Niall Quinn. The thirty-five-year-old centre forward had amassed a record number of goals for Ireland during his sixteen-year international career but now, after eighty-eight caps, his days appeared to be numbered.

The man affectionately dubbed 'Quinninho' by Sunderland fans was anything but bitter, though. If it was good for Ireland, it was good enough for him. He was happy just 'lending a helping hand', he told the *Mirror*, and seemed just as excited as anyone about the team's youthful attacking combo.

'It's added a whole new dimension now to when Mick McCarthy took over,' Quinn said. 'We were definitely a big-man–small-man team and Damien has come in for us and the job he does is immense. Damien is world-class, without a doubt. He's turning world-class players inside out, every time he plays for Ireland. We saw some of the turns he did the other night against Russia and the positions he got himself into – if he does that on the world stage, he could go anywhere really.'

While McCarthy seemed intent on using Duff as a central raider, debate lingered elsewhere as to the Blackburn man's best position. Should his devilish advances be subjected to opposing full-backs or centre-halves? Duff, as you would expect, just wanted to play. Anywhere.

'Mick has so many options going for him that the top priority for us all will be just to get into the squad,' he said in the *Sunday Mirror*.

'Anything after that is a plus. But it's a bit too early to speculate on who's going to get into the team. The highlight of my Ireland career so far was to score against Croatia, and the fact that it came when I was playing through the middle makes you think that that's the place you want to be.

'But the competition there is every bit as tough as it is on the left side of midfield and, in that situation, you're grateful to fill any role the manager offers you – even in goal!'

Six days before his twenty-third birthday, on 24 February 2002, Damien Duff played in the biggest game of his club career. On offer that day was not only the first major domestic prize of the season but also a place in the UEFA Cup, and, to claim both, Blackburn – playing in a League Cup final for the first time – would have to beat Tottenham Hotspur, three-times winners of the competition and a club with a proud cup tradition both at home and in Europe.

Tottenham were heavily fancied to lift the trophy in Cardiff and it was easy to work out why. Glenn Hoddle's side boasted a wealth of big-game experience, thanks to the presence of seasoned internationals such as Teddy Sheringham, Christian Ziege, Gus Poyet and Les Ferdinand, and were sitting ten places above Blackburn in the Premiership table.

Another factor in installing the north London side as favourites was the manner in which they'd demolished Chelsea in the semi-finals, winning 5–1 at White Hart Lane to overturn comprehensively a 2–1 first leg deficit.

Souness was happy for his team to adopt the role of underdogs, and continued to stress emphatically that winning the cup was firmly ensconced below Premiership survival on Rovers' list of priorities. He knew exactly what his players were capable of on their day, and was quite content to see the extra pressure created by the expectancy of winning being heaped onto the shoulders of Hoddle's ageing outfit.

For Blackburn, the game also represented a welcome distraction from their faltering league campaign, and Duff – whom both managers identified as a potential match winner ahead of the contest – was aware that a Rovers victory could revive their Premiership fortunes.

'I think we're a better team than our current place in the

table indicates, and hopefully we'll prove it at Cardiff,' he said in the *News of the World*. 'A trophy would work wonders for our self-belief, and maybe make all the difference in moving us towards the middle of the Premiership table.

'More than anything, I'd love to do well if given the chance of playing in the World Cup finals. And I reckon I'd be in better shape to handle the pressures knowing Blackburn's Premiership future is secured.'

Souness, who won the League Cup four times as a Liverpool player in the early 1980s, knew that Duff could play a key role in extending his manager's glorious association with the competition. 'Even before I came to this club I knew [Damien] was a special kind of player. And he's proved it with some brilliant performances,' said Souness.

'We need Damien playing well at Cardiff. Tottenham can be difficult to break down if they're given the time to settle. We must try to get behind them down the flanks to create chances.'

The final, played in front of more than 72,000 under the roof of Cardiff's Millennium Stadium, was an absorbing affair packed with drama at both ends. And, at the end of it, it was the blue and white hordes that had travelled down from Lancashire who were celebrating.

Matt Jansen and Christian Ziege exchanged first-half goals to ensure the scores remained level at the break, before Andy Cole pounced for a sixty-ninth-minute winner, and man-of - the-match Brad Friedel kept Tottenham at bay with a string of outstanding saves.

Blackburn's seventy-four-year wait for major cup success was over, and the identity of Rovers' winning-goal hero ensured the press had a field day. During his time in charge of the national team Glenn Hoddle, reporters gleefully remembered, left Cole out of England's 1998 World Cup squad after suggesting that the striker needed 'four or five chances' to score.

The papers lapped it up, with REVENGE IS SOU SWEET FOR COLE (*Daily Record*), STUFF YOU HOD (*Sun*) and ANGRY COLE GETS EVEN (*Daily Star*) among the following day's headlines.

Damien Duff was not the name hogging those headlines, but the part he played in securing the first major prize of his career should never be overlooked, according to Henry Winter of the *Daily Telegraph*. He wrote, 'Damien Duff was showing what a fine future stretches out before him. His was a terrific all-round performance, containing eye-catching work at both ends, creating and covering in equal measure.'

As an eventful campaign entered its final phase, there was no telling how their Worthington Cup triumph would affect the remainder of Blackburn's season. Would the achievement spark a huge surge of confidence, providing the team with the momentum necessary to pull them away from trouble at the foot of the Premiership? Or would the players simply settle for landing one piece of major silverware and struggle to motivate themselves for a series of high-pressure relegation battles?

The first signs of an answer were not long in coming, and it was good news for Rovers fans. A draw at Bolton was followed by a resounding 3–0 win at home to Aston Villa in which David Dunn, Damien Duff and Andy Cole all found a way past Villa keeper Peter Schmeichel to ease the pressure at Ewood Park.

Rather than dwell on the three points just gained, Duff was more concerned with grabbing a large share of the thirty still on offer from Blackburn's final ten games. He told the press after the match, 'We can't get too carried away with the Villa result because really it was just the start for us if we're to stay up. We've given ourselves a lifeline with that win, but the fact remains that we're still down there because we've had a dodgy three or four months.

'There are ten games to go now, and, to be absolutely sure, I believe we'll have to win half of them. It was a huge win over Aston Villa, but there's no escaping the significance of our next game, at home to Ipswich. That is massive, the ultimate six-pointer, and when you consider we also have crucial matches coming up against Leicester, Everton, Southampton and Middlesbrough, it's easy to appreciate the job that still needs doing.'

Goalscorer Duff also paid tribute to Dean Saunders, the former striker who enjoyed a prolific career with Wales and a string of clubs including Derby County, Liverpool, Aston Villa and Galatasaray, and who was now coaching the forwards at Blackburn.

'I'm really enjoying working under Dean, even though he always seems to be on my case,' Duff continued. 'He keeps stressing that I should get in the box and score more goals and his influence is definitely paying off. It was nice for me and for him, too, to bag that one against Villa.'

Duff seemed at times to be showing signs of fatigue as the Villa match wore on, although his naturally sloping shoulders would often give the false impression that he was feeling the pace. On this occasion, even the gaffer was deceived.

'As for Duffer, in the first half he caused them immense problems, then in the second looked as though he had been shot, he was so tired,' said Souness. 'But, when it looks as though he's down and out, he finds a burst of energy from somewhere.'

Finding energy was blatantly not a problem for Duff when fellow strugglers Ipswich rolled up at Ewood Park for, in his opinion, 'the ultimate six-pointer'.

After bursting past three defenders he buried a low shot beyond the helpless visiting keeper Matteo Sereni to open the scoring and guarantee his entry into March's Goal of the Month competition. Andy Cole was also on target – again – as Rovers secured a significant 2–1 victory that saw them creep out of the relegation zone.

Having taken seven points from three games to breathe life into what had been a pretty abject league campaign, there was no doubt that Blackburn's Worthington Cup heroics had had a galvanising effect on the club.

Cole, who was about to start a three-match suspension having been sent off at Bolton, had proved to be a fine signing. But the man-of-the-moment tag belonged to Duff, with his goalscoring displays against Villa and Ipswich – not to mention the fact that Blackburn's Premiership safety was far from assured – leading to yet more transfer talk.

Fulham were the latest club to express an interest

according to the *People* and, as a result, Blackburn were willing to double Duff's £15,000-a-week deal in order to keep him at the club. The way the Ballyboden flyer was performing, it would surely be money well spent.

CHAPTER 7

Domestic Bliss

'Niall Quinn, sitting beside me in the dug-out, turned
to me after just three minutes and said that Damien had
already won the man-of-the-match award.'

MICK MCCARTHY, MARCH 2002

'He reminds me of our own Brian Laudrup. You know
he is going to get the ball, you know he is going to
keep the ball but you don't know how to get the ball back off
him. That is the sign of a truly great player.'

Those were the words of Denmark coach Morten Olsen,
voiced moments after his side had been methodically ripped
to shreds by the subject of his tribute, Damien Duff. With the
start of the World Cup just two months away, Ireland's big
secret was out.

Denmark's visit to Dublin at the end of March had given
Mick McCarthy another opportunity to gauge at first hand
how his players were shaping up ahead of the summer's big
event. McCarthy had already decided on the majority of his
twenty-three-man squad for Japan & South Korea, but a
friendly meeting with fellow World Cup contestants

Denmark provided a contingent of fringe players with the chance to promote themselves from 'maybes' to 'definites'.

Duff was not among that contingent of fringe players with a point to prove but decided to outshine everyone else, anyway. Having been restored to the left wing to allow Clinton Morrison a rare start in attack, Duff conjured up a scintillating display of old-fashioned wing play, setting up Ian Harte for the opening goal in a 3–0 win and turning the Danish defence – right-back Thomas Rytter in particular – inside out.

Not for the first time in his career, Duff was compared to the great George Best – this time by former Ireland manager Eoin Hand – while others rated the display as the most electrifying witnessed at Lansdowne Road for many years.

Six minutes from the end of the match, Duff was withdrawn, prompting 42,000 people to rise to their feet and heartily show their appreciation. The applause had barely died down by the time Big Mick and his boys began engaging in the post-match analysis. Most of the talk, inevitably, centred on one man.

'Damien Duff plays a physically demanding game and excels in one-against-one situations,' said Mick McCarthy. 'He was outstanding against the Danes tonight. Niall Quinn, sitting beside me in the dug-out, turned to me after just three minutes and said that Damien had already won the man-of-the-match award. How right he was!'

Robbie Keane paid tribute: 'I put him up there with the Ryan Giggs and Harry Kewells of this world. It's great playing alongside Damien.'

Meanwhile, Irish veteran Steve Staunton said: 'Damien has the world at his feet. He's going to be a big star at the World Cup. It's not very nice marking him, I know from club football. The world's at the boy's feet at the moment and unfortunately for some of us in England he's only going to get better, but for Ireland it's great.'

Speaking at greater length about the specific threat that Duff posed was defender Kenny Cunningham. Having faced the Blackburn man several times on the domestic scene while playing for Wimbledon, Cunningham could reveal from first-hand experience just why it was so difficult for defenders to deal with his impish international colleague.

Addressing reporters after the game, Cunningham said, 'I've always found it difficult to play against him. You've got to be so clever to keep him quiet and if you're left isolated you're in real trouble. He has a low centre of gravity, he drops his shoulders, leans in and then glides past you. He's so elusive, he seems to have rubber hips and he can get you off balance very easily. With other players, you hope to have some physical contact which can upset them but you can't do that with Damien. He does appear to have a lower centre of gravity than any other player I know.

'Perhaps he could go to another league. That would be Damien's decision. But, if he continues to progress at his current rate, there may well be an opportunity for him to go elsewhere. Class is class, whatever league you're in. Damien's got the ability and the strength of character to play in any league in the world. The World Cup's a great stage to prove how good you are, and all the major clubs from around the globe will be there waving their chequebooks so you never know what might happen.

'It's a dilemma as to where to play Damien – up front or on the left – but it's a great dilemma to have. But when he's on the left he can beat people and get some great crosses in. I'm just glad I don't have to face him.'

It wasn't just Ireland's current crop of players who were queuing up to sing the praises of their red-hot Rover. Johnny Giles, the former Manchester United and Leeds midfielder, is widely regarded as one of the greatest players ever to have represented the Republic of Ireland.

In his *Daily Mail* column, published two days after Ireland's victory over Denmark, Giles enthused over Duff's exceptional dismantling of the Danes. He suggested that Roy and Robbie Keane were no longer the only two players capable of single-handedly inspiring the Irish team, and that Duff's ample skills would soon see him rated alongside Robert Pires, Harry Kewell and Ryan Giggs as one of the game's finest wingers. He wrote: 'After making a goal for Ian Harte and generally tormenting the Danish defence, Duff heard himself being described as the next George Best. A modest lad, he will treat such speculation as the mythology it is. But hopefully he will draw much confidence from the aura he created on Wednesday. Certainly, I've seen enough of him to know that he has the capacity to make an impact at the highest level. He has a wonderful knack of making the game look easy.'

The only problem with Duff's outstanding form was the widespread acclaim it was attracting. That meant that any hopes Ireland had of using Duff as their World Cup secret weapon had all but vanished. Everyone was now talking about a player in the form of his life following a series of magical displays for club and country, and Mick McCarthy reluctantly admitted that he could no longer be considered an unknown quantity.

Denmark boss Olsen, who captained a fine Danish team at the 1986 World Cup, was also aware of the situation. But he did offer some words of comfort. 'The problem for Damien Duff and Ireland is that the world now knows all about him, the element of surprise is gone from his game now and teams will know what to expect come the World Cup finals,' he said. 'The good thing for Ireland is that he is still a very difficult player to mark.'

Not everyone was waxing lyrical about Duffer's latest wonder show, though. In a quiet corner of Lancashire one man was far from happy. His club were about to play two crucial games in the space of three days as they battled for their Premiership lives, and one of the team's most influential players was knackered due to the exhausting exertions of his extended midweek run-out. Graeme Souness was fuming.

'I was thinking of ringing [Mick McCarthy] beforehand to ask whether Damien could play for no more than forty-five minutes – but I decided not to bother, thinking common sense would prevail,' he said.

'Then the lad is left on almost to the bitter end – which is hardly fair on Damien or Blackburn, especially because this was only a friendly. Damien is prone to hamstring strains –

especially when he's tired – as are many players, including the likes of Ryan Giggs.

'We have two vital games in three days, so what are we left with now – the prospect of playing him for no more than an hour in either? It's unfair and it would appear that there's one rule for some clubs and one rule for others. Some managers ring up to say their player has a strain and pull him out. Other managers ring up with the same information only to be told to send the player along so that the international team's doctor can have a look.'

McCarthy moved quickly to defend himself. 'It doesn't bother me,' he said in the *Mirror*. 'I have my priorities and he has his. If managers pick up the phone and ask me to consider their position or situation, I do it within reason. But if they don't, what I am supposed to do? Bobby Robson expressed his concerns about Shay [Given] playing. I was quite happy to use other keepers and leave out Shay. The difference is that Bobby picked up the phone to talk to me. That's what any boss should do if they have a problem.'

Unfortunately for Souness, the condition of Duff wasn't his only concern ahead of his team's pivotal meetings with Leicester and Southampton. While on international duty, Duff had been quizzed in a press conference about the prospect of relegation for Blackburn and how that would affect his future. His comments were pounced upon and, the day before Rovers' trip to Filbert Street, several newspapers suggested that, should Blackburn go down, Duff would be heading straight for the Ewood Park exit.

'The Premiership is the place to be so I'd have to look at

the situation if we went down,' Duff was reported to have said. 'I spent two seasons in the First Division and it's a horrible league to play in. I don't want to go back to it because, to play international football, you must be playing in the Premiership.'

That prompted the Sunday tabloids to suggest that Arsène Wenger was now tracking the player, with Arsenal supposedly preparing a £12 million summer raid.

Duff, no doubt, would have been desperate to put the club-versus-country row and transfer speculation behind him by getting back onto the pitch, the environment in which he had always seemed most comfortable. His return to action was delayed, though, as Souness decided that his international exploits had left him in no fit state to face the Premiership's bottom side Leicester.

After the game, which Blackburn lost 2–1, to leave them precariously placed above the drop zone, Souness explained why he had chosen not to include Duff. 'He turned up knackered on Friday,' said Souness. 'Thanks, Ireland I'm not happy about the situation. My argument is it is in the best interests of Mick McCarthy and my interests to look after the player.'

Blackburn did welcome Duff back for the April Fools' Day clash with Southampton – and how they needed him! By the time of the evening kick-off at Ewood Park, results earlier that day had seen Rovers drop into the bottom three. They didn't stay there for long, though, and for that, predictably, they were thankful to their returning left-winger.

In what was fast becoming a trademark move, Duff cut in

from the left before scoring with a low, drilled shot to edge the home side in front in the twenty-seventh minute, and moments later he crossed for Spanish striker Yordi to head the second goal in a priceless 2–0 win for Rovers.

It was the perfect response from a player who had begun the match with question marks over both his future and his physical condition. In a clear display of loyalty to his only ever professional club, Duff celebrated his goal with great vigour, wildly whipping off his shirt and kissing the red rose badge.

Afterwards Duff told Sky Sports, 'I didn't feel fresh today, especially in the second half, but we battled well and just nicked it with two good goals. We've been dominating games all season and just giving away sloppy goals. Of course we're confident of beating the drop. I experienced relegation with the club two years ago and I don't want to go through that again.'

Souness admitted he was pleased to see Duff complete the match, having not trained at all since returning to the club from Ireland because he'd been experiencing flu-like symptoms. 'We have given him three or four pints of Guinness every day and he did very well to last the game,' joked the relieved Blackburn boss.

Duff had emerged as an inspirational figure in Blackburn's battle to beat the drop – and in Ireland's pre-World Cup programme – and the tabloids were loving it. Headlines such as DUFFED UP, DUFF AT THE TOP and THE RIGHT S-DUFF were all getting a regular airing, and rumours of a move away from Blackburn just would not go away.

Sunderland boss Peter Reid went public with his

admiration for the player, claiming, 'Duff is a quality player and, if he was to become available, he's someone I would be interested in.' The *Sunday Mirror* reckoned that Liverpool, Newcastle and Celtic were locked in a three-way battle for his signature. Just for good measure, the name of Chelsea was also thrown into the mix by the *Independent*.

Mid-April saw Ireland's World Cup preparations continue with a home friendly against another team on its way to Japan & South Korea, the USA.

As an increasing number of managers around Britain were supposedly preparing to make a move for Duff, the two bosses who already had him at their disposal seemed to be getting along fine again. The dispute that had been triggered by Duff's last international appearance seemed to have been resolved, with Mick McCarthy stating there was 'no problem at all' between him and Graeme Souness.

Having terrorised Denmark from the left flank in that previous outing, Duff was reunited in attack with Robbie Keane, while Kevin Kilbane was assigned to patrol the left-hand side of midfield.

'I watch them in training and they're a terrific partnership,' McCarthy said about the Duff–Keane combo in front of the assembled press. 'They have a great understanding. Their pace, their skill and their mobility will frighten defences in the World Cup. They are difficult to deal with as a few decent teams have found out – like Denmark.

'People will say, "You don't have a big fella up there", but we like to get the ball down and play now. When Duff and

Keane play up there they find the angles and create space – not only for each other but for others.

'As a former centre-half, I know I would far rather the right-back was picking up someone with Duff's pace and skill than have him bearing down on me. Damien is quite happy to switch from what people might say is his normal position.'

Blocking Ireland's path to goal was the ample frame of Duff's Blackburn teammate Brad Friedel. The US goalkeeper would be giving away nothing during the game, but was happy to dish out compliments beforehand.

'Maybe only Ryan Giggs is better [than Duff] in the Premiership at the moment and that's mainly because of his age and experience,' Friedel said in the *Mirror*.

'But Damien is as good as anyone going down the left. He will show in the World Cup that he is best in that position. That will not only be for the tournament but for years to come. I should know, I play with him every day.'

The match was something of a washout, with torrential rain making conditions almost unplayable as Ireland won 2–1 thanks to Gary Doherty's late strike. In the crowd at Lansdowne Road was Phil Thompson, Liverpool's assistant manager, who had travelled to Dublin to cast his eye over a player whom Anfield boss Gérard Houllier – if reports were to be believed – was extremely keen on adding to his squad.

It proved to be something of a wasted trip for Thompson. Duff's scampering style was completely unsuited to the atrocious conditions, with his ability to run at defenders hampered by the puddle-strewn surface. Also, Duff was playing as a striker and not in the position that Liverpool were interested in strengthening – the left wing. And he was taken off at half-time. At least one Liverpool legend – Souness – was happy.

The subject of Duff's best position in the national team and also his future at club level were frequent topics of discussion. Kevin Kilbane was glad to engage in both. 'I just hope that Mick plays Damien in an attacking role, otherwise I won't be in the team,' Kilbane told reporters after the game.

'However, if I lose my place I won't resent anyone. Damien's a tremendous player, a great character and a friend. I think he's even better in training – he likes to nutmeg us all. No matter where he plays – on the left, on the right or down the middle – the lad is awesome. With his talent, I wouldn't be surprised at all if he moved in the summer.

'We're probably coming to a stage where Blackburn have to think to themselves, "Are we going to cash in on him or are we going to keep him?" – and offer him big, big money to stay. In my eyes he would be sensational for Liverpool and would relish being involved in the big games, pushing for the title or in the Champions League.'

Even Duff's international teammates were talking up a lucrative move away from Blackburn. Souness was having none of it, though, stating emphatically that his most prized possession – who still had two years left on his contract – was going nowhere.

'We have not been contacted by anyone about selling Damien Duff,' Souness told the press on the eve of Blackburn's Premiership trip to Middlesbrough. 'He's not for sale. We're in a very, very fortunate position because we're not a selling club. So he's not going anywhere, end of story.

For some members of the press Souness's message obviously didn't register, with Leeds apparently joining the growing list of interested parties.

When Duff returned to domestic duty, for that away day at Middlesbrough, he demonstrated once again just why he was the subject of so much hype. After embarking on a mazy run that seemed to leave the entire Boro defence in a daze, Duff crossed for Yordi to break the deadlock, and then took the corner from which Andy Cole doubled Rovers' lead.

Chants of 'Staying up, staying up, staying up' from Blackburn's travelling contingent greeted their team's 3–1 triumph, and on this evidence it was hard to disagree.

Duff, understandably for a man never at ease in the media spotlight, was keen to play down the rave reviews that his excellent form had merited. When the hacks caught up with him after the game he was typically economical with his words.

'I've improved over the season but I don't let it get to me. And, if I did, my family would bring me down to earth... With the World Cup around the corner, I hope I'm not peaking too early... As for being linked with Liverpool, Leeds and Celtic, I don't let that sort of thing get to me... The most important thing in my sights is Blackburn Rovers and that's all I'm worried about.'

Those three points at Boro, plus another one gained from a 2–2 draw in their following game at home to Newcastle, meant that by the time Rovers played Everton at the end of April their Premiership safety was already assured. With three games left, Blackburn could finally relax.

Although too modest ever to admit it himself, Duff could reflect on the campaign with a huge amount of satisfaction, having made an immense contribution to Rovers' fight for survival. In doing so, he had comprehensively wiped away the miserable memories of his last Premiership experience. Back then, under Brian Kidd, the youthful Duff had been restricted to a peripheral role as Blackburn crashed out of the top-flight just four years after winning it.

Now, though, he had come of age, consistently reminding the footballing public why so many had tipped him for stardom earlier on in his career.

With Blackburn's Premiership safety confirmed, Duff felt it was time to put the record straight about his future plans – and it didn't make good reading for the chasing pack of potential bidders.

'I am happy, especially now that we are safe in the Premiership for next season and we have European football to look forward to after the Worthington Cup win,' he said in the *Express*.

'I haven't heard anything from Blackburn or Liverpool – it's all speculation. And I am in no rush to do anything about my future or to go anywhere. I am at a great club with a great set of lads and a great manager, so there is no reason for me to want to leave.

'Blackburn Rovers is part of my life. I am a loyal sort of person and I will not be going anywhere. The Premiership is the place to be, I have had a great year playing in it and I would have been devastated if we had gone down. We have a young set of players at Blackburn now and the future is very bright.'

He also revealed to the *Sun* that his head was not about to be turned by the big bucks and bright lights of Serie A or La Liga.

'I would not be into moving to another country. Not at all. I don't really take to the sun very well. I found playing in the World Youth Cup in Nigeria three years ago very difficult because of the heat. I don't think moving to a hot country – either now or in the future – would be a good idea for me.

'I wouldn't really fancy learning a new language either and I can't see myself leaving England, to be honest. But, despite what has been said, I have not heard anything from Blackburn about a long-term contract. I have two seasons left, but I would be more than happy to talk to the club about a longer deal.'

Blackburn still had the formalities of the Premiership season to complete, with two games left to play. The first of those, away to Liverpool, gave the club supposedly as intent as anyone on luring Duff away from Ewood Park the chance to have a close look at their prime target. Graeme Souness may have been secretly hoping for Duff to have a quiet night in order to dampen the Reds' interest, but the man himself had other ideas. Duff was, after all, 'on fire', according to his boss, and there were no signs of his cooling down just yet as he played a double one-two deep into Liverpool territory before levelling the scores at 1–1 in a thrilling game that Rovers eventually lost 4–3.

Despite Duff's statement that he would 'not be going anywhere', speculation regarding his future was still rife. Manchester United – one of the few clubs in the top half of the Premiership who hadn't yet been linked with the

Blackburn winger – were now reportedly interested, and news of Blackburn's pursuit of United striker Dwight Yorke had further fuelled rumours of a Duff switch to Old Trafford.

Speaking to the *Mirror*, Souness attempted to clear up the situation. 'There's nothing in that,' he said. 'I've not spoken to anyone from Manchester United in regard to Damien Duff. We've made an enquiry and asked for a price for Dwight Yorke and we've been told that price, which is too much for us. But there has never been any mention of Damien Duff in that deal.'

The final day of the season saw Fulham visit Ewood Park. On another memorable afternoon for Duff he was presented with Blackburn's Player of the Year trophy before kick-off and then scored in 3–0 win that helped Rovers secure a highly respectable tenth-place Premiership finish.

The strike took Duff's tally for the season to seven Premiership goals (in thirty-two appearances), in addition to the one he scored in the Worthington Cup. After the game, he once again took the opportunity to pledge his allegiance to the Blackburn cause.

'I have been here since I was 16 and I feel I have been improving all the time,' he told the Press Association. 'It's nice to be linked with other clubs, it shows you are doing well, but I love it at Blackburn. We are in Europe and in the Premiership, we have a great manager, we have a very young squad with top players such as David Dunn and Matt Jansen and hopefully we can go on to better things next year.

'Please God, I will be here next season. I love it here and I don't want to go anywhere. I have a lot of friends here, the lads are great, and once I am settled somewhere I want to stay – that's the type of guy I am.'

Duff wanted to stay then, and Blackburn had no intention of letting him go. The Ewood Park club's desire to keep him, however, would be severely tested following the events of the coming summer.

CHAPTER 8

Great Expectations

'I don't suppose many other countries will know
that much yet of Damien Duff. They will do very soon.'
ROY KEANE, MAY 2002

T he history of the World Cup is littered with heroes, villains, drama and controversy, and in 2002 the Republic of Ireland managed to uphold every single one of those traditions. Leaving Japan & South Korea with memories more enduring than those generated by previous Irish World Cup teams was never going to be easy, but somehow Mick McCarthy and his men managed to achieve it. Just not the way that anyone had quite imagined.

Unfortunately for Ireland, it seemed that, at one stage, they were contributing to all the wrong categories. There were certainly villains, or at least *a* villain, depending on which side of the fence you were placed as one of the most astonishing episodes in recent World Cup history unfolded before a ball had been kicked.

With it came enough drama and controversy to last the

whole tournament, and probably several more after that too. But while the extraordinary 'will-he-stay-or-will-he-go?' saga raged on around team captain Roy Keane – a man who many felt was Ireland's only player of genuine world class – the nation yearned for a ray of light to brighten a campaign seemingly heading for disaster before it had begun.

They were crying out for heroes. Luckily, they weren't long in coming.

Having created some glorious memories at their two previous World Cup finals appearances, Ireland headed to the Far East confident that they could once again upset some of the game's reputed big hitters. After all, that was exactly what they'd done in 1990 and 1994.

In Italia '90 Jack Charlton's men took their place at football's top table for the very first time and were considered little more than rank outsiders, especially after the draw for the first stage saw them grouped with the much-fancied England and Holland (just as they had been, ironically, at the European Championships in 1988).

Glued to the TV set back in Ballyboden was an eleven-year-old Damien Duff. 'I remember watching those European Championships in Germany (in 1988) and then every second of the World Cup two years later,' he has since recalled. 'It was a wonderful experience.'

To the young Duff's delight, a low drive struck by the trusty left foot of his favourite player, Kevin Sheedy, cancelled out Gary Lineker's early opener to earn Ireland a point from their first game against England. And after drawing again in their second match – this time a drab 0–0 stalemate with Egypt – just one team were left standing in their way of a place in the last sixteen.

Trouble was, that team contained the likes of Marco van Basten, Ruud Gullit, Frank Rijkaard and Ronald Koeman. They were a team who two years earlier had landed a major title – something that somehow eluded the brilliant Dutch team of the previous generation – when they won the European Championships in Germany in emphatic style. By 1990 many were tipping Holland to add the World Cup to their European title.

Big Jack's men had other ideas, though. While the Ireland squad list could hardly be considered 'star-studded' next to that of their more illustrious opponents, Charlton did have a number of players at his disposal who enjoyed significant success at club level, such as Packie Bonner, Ray Houghton, Ronnie Whelan, Paul McGrath, Steve Staunton and John Aldridge.

And, having fostered an unerring spirit among his team, Charlton boasted a side who believed they could compete with anything the tournament had to offer.

Trailing to Ruud Gullit's expertly executed first-half goal as the match drifted into its final phase, Ireland were in desperate need of a saviour and found one in the unlikely form of Niall Quinn, the twenty-three-year-old Manchester City striker who had featured for a total of just six minutes in Ireland's first two matches before Charlton handed him a starting role against the Dutch.

He responded in perfect fashion, reacting the fastest in the seventy-first minute to pounce on a loose ball and slide in an equaliser that sent Ireland's travelling legion of supporters – and the watching nation back home – wild.

It was a goal that the Irish author Roddy Doyle for one is unlikely to forget. Describing the feelings evoked by that 1–1 draw in the book *My Favourite Year*, Doyle wrote, 'I was glad I was Irish, proud of it. I'd never felt that way before; I'd have been embarrassed to. Not now, though. I was Irish and it was a wonderful thing to be.'

The fairytale wasn't to end there. Romania were next up, and, after a goalless 120 minutes in Genoa, Packie Bonner's shootout save from Daniel Timofte meant that, if David O'Leary was successful from the spot, then Ireland were through. A brief pause, a considered approach and a composed side-foot finish later, Ireland were in the quarter-finals of the World Cup.

There, the great adventure was ended – just – by hosts Italy, who edged a tense affair in Rome thanks to a single goal from the tournament's surprise star Toto Schillaci.

But, while the immediate dream was over, the effect of the team's notable run on an awe-struck generation of Irish boys would be long-lasting. Young lads with aspirations of one day wearing the emerald green – the Damien Duffs, the Robbie Keanes and the Shay Givens – watched starry-eyed as those lofty ambitions were fortified by the achievements of the team that Jack built, idols to a man.

The European Championships victory over England in 1988 may have signalled the beginning of a memorable era for Irish football, but never before had Ireland appeared at the game's most prestigious gathering, let alone made it through to the later stages. Now, a new breed of fledglings had been inspired to follow suit.

One of that breed was Shay Given, who was fourteen years old when he and his family gathered nervously around the television at home in Lifford, County Donegal, to watch the penalty shootout triumph over Romania.

'It was a fantastic occasion,' he recalled, in the *Daily Telegraph*. 'At that stage I had not decided to become a keeper. But that night I went into the back garden to play football with my brothers and pretended to be Packie Bonner.

'It was one of those moments in sport where everyone can look back and say where they were when Packie made that save. From that point on every lad in Ireland wanted to be a footballer.'

Four years later Jack's boys were back on the big stage in America, when Ray Houghton's looping winner against eventual finalists Italy helped Ireland through to the second round, where they were beaten 2–0 by Holland.

Now, in 2002, Ireland were contenders again. It was a chance for the more senior members of Mick McCarthy's squad – Quinn, Steve Staunton, Gary Kelly, Roy Keane and Jason McAteer – to enhance their World Cup memories by adding to their experiences of 1990 and 1994. For other, more fresh-faced members of the party, it was a chance to emulate heroes of the past and inspire the nation's youth, just as they themselves had been inspired a few years earlier.

Ireland's first-stage opponents would be Cameroon, Germany and Saudi Arabia following a draw that had left all four teams in Group E relatively satisfied. For Ireland it could certainly have been worse, and some even speculated that the challenge presented by Portugal and Holland in the qualifying phase was more testing than anything their group opponents at the finals would muster.

That line of thinking was based on the theory that Saudi Arabia were one of the weakest teams in the tournament and Cameroon were potentially dangerous but definitely beatable. Germany, traditionally one of the competition's leading powers, were a team whom everybody *had* wanted to avoid at the World Cup – until now.

A dreadful showing at Euro 2000 was followed by a stuttering World Cup qualifying campaign that was scarred by a stunning 5–1 defeat at home to England. In the end, Rudi Voller's side had needed a play-off to beat Ukraine and claim a place at the finals. This German side, critics announced, was the poorest in living memory.

Duff, echoing the reaction of several other members of the Irish camp in the *News of the World*, was pleased with the draw. Not quite as pleased as Germany's former World Cup-winner Paul Breitner – 'This is an early Christmas present for us,' he proclaimed – but quietly confident that his team would make it beyond the initial stage.

'I think all the lads will be confident that we can at least make the second phase of the competition,' said Duff, who admitted after the December draw that he didn't know a great deal about Cameroon, apart from Roger Milla, and that Mick McCarthy had already done his homework on Saudi Arabia because they'd been potential opponents for Ireland at the play-off stage.

'A few years ago, we might have had some fears about taking on Germany. They had such a good record in World Cup and European Championship finals. But they've been on a downer in recent times and we will feel confident.

'We shouldn't really have any fears about facing a team like Germany after our performances against Portugal and Holland in the qualifiers, which we went through with seven wins and three draws in 10 games.'

Duff's majestic form in the second half of the 2001–2 season scuppered any hopes he may have had of ambling into the World Cup unnoticed. He'd helped etch the name of Blackburn Rovers onto a major cup for the first time in almost seventy-five years and then acted as the catalyst for the club's Premiership survival surge, comfortably bagging Rovers' Player of the Year award in the process.

On the international stage, he was now consistently delivering the sort of dashing performances that his teenage precocity had promised. Consequently, as the World Cup approached, Duff featured heavily in the pre-tournament press coverage. His name often appeared in ones-to-watch-at-the-World-Cup articles, with some predicting that his stock would rise significantly on the back of a decent showing in the competition, just as that of Norman Whiteside, David Platt, Paul Gascoigne and Michael Owen had done in previous years.

It seemed that everyone was onto Ireland's not-so-secret-weapon. Even Canada's *Montreal Gazette* picked him out as a potential star, claiming that Duff had 'shown enough in the qualifying campaign to suggest he can take on the world'.

A whole array of players and managers were at it too. Graeme Souness chimed in: 'Playing in the World Cup finals is a huge challenge for any young player but it helps when you know you're capable of competing with the best. Damien's got that kind of talent.'

Legend George Best picked his star players: 'When Jack Charlton retired as the manager, we thought that would be the end, but Mick McCarthy has done unbelievably well. They're lucky having Roy Keane, Robbie Keane and Damien Duff.'

And Niall Quinn confidently asserted Duff's impending stardom: 'This competition could be tailor-made for Damien Duff to burst on to the world stage. He played up front for Ireland for the first time against Holland and destroyed Jaap Stam when we beat them at Lansdowne Road. A couple of repeat performances in the World Cup would probably bring him to superstar status.'

'We have a few players who are capable of causing surprises,' revealed Roy Keane. 'I don't suppose many other countries will know that much yet of Damien Duff. They will do very soon. Players like him will be going out to games without any fear, ready to express themselves.'

As the growing band of Duff fans continued to acclaim their man, the subject of their adulation was getting a little uncomfortable with the pressure he now found himself under. No longer an unknown quantity who could rely on the surprise element to startle opponents, Duff was becoming a marked man. Big things were expected of him each time he stepped onto the pitch, whether it was in the green of Ireland or the blue-and-white halves of Blackburn Rovers.

It was a situation he discussed with the press when he visited Dublin to launch a new Adidas Predator boot shortly before the World Cup finals. 'Every man and his dog seems to be making a prediction about what I am going to do at the World Cup and I am getting a little p**d off,' he was reported as saying in the *Sun*.

'I understand that people get excited when a World Cup is around the corner but people are saying I'm going to do this and I'm going to do that. It is good in a way that I am getting so much hype and attention but I am kind of sick of it because it is putting pressure on me. When people predict that you will do great things then everyone expects you to do it and it doesn't always work out like that.'

It was an interesting insight into the mind of a twenty-three-year-old player whose private nature meant that he was rarely found addressing the media at great length. On this occasion, though, he was happy to express his views on a number of topics.

Regarding the popular debate over his best position, he admitted first and foremost that he didn't care where he was playing as long as he was lining up in Mick McCarthy's starting XI. He did, though, stress that he felt more comfortable operating out on the wing. That was where he'd spent the vast majority of his playing career, and the areas in which he caused opponents most distress were usually down the flanks rather than in the penalty box. In addition to that, his goalscoring record at international level – one goal in twenty-five appearances – was by no means prolific.

By his own admission he didn't possess the natural instinct

in front of goal that Robbie Keane and Clinton Morrison were blessed with, but, along with Roy Keane, Matt Holland and Mark Kinsella, he was among a band of players capable of supplementing the strikers' contribution with a few goals.

Unfortunately for Duff's good friend and strike partner Robbie Keane, his irregular involvement at Leeds meant that he wasn't exactly firing on all cylinders as the World Cup approached. Not a problem, though, according to Duff. 'If I was a manager I would pick Robbie Keane every week, I would always find him a place somewhere in the team,' he told the *Sunday Mirror*.

'And I know for a fact that he is coming good in time for the World Cup. I know how good he is and how good he makes it for people playing alongside him. I can't wait, to be honest.'

Duff also spoke of the 'horrors' he had gone through at Blackburn, when his form dipped during the tenure of Brian Kidd and his subsequent loss of confidence cost him his place at international level.

Now, though, having come through the experience, he was a better player than the one who had suffered the pain of relegation with Rovers three years earlier. Duff was grateful for the loyalty shown to him by the ever-trusting Mick McCarthy and Graeme Souness, and having smoothed out the rough edges of his game he was now a more mature footballer revelling in the added responsibility that came with being one of the most established members of the Ewood Park playing staff. Not that he felt equally well established in the international setup.

'I'm still the young pup when it comes to international football,' he said. 'I may be the longest-serving player with Blackburn but it's different with Ireland.'

Fans were given the chance to bid an excited farewell to Mick McCarthy's squad at Lansdowne Road on 16 May, when Ireland entertained one of England's World Cup group opponents, Nigeria, the day before they headed off to the Far East.

It wasn't the send-off they were hoping for, though, as Nigeria won a relatively tame affair – the players' main objective, understandably, was to avoid injury so close to the main event – and in the process ruined an impressive record that had seen Ireland go two years without losing on home turf.

McCarthy had fielded his strongest possible starting XI. But, despite seeing his side slip to a 2–1 defeat, the Ireland boss remained upbeat, insisting that he would take 'more positives than negatives' out of the performance.

That starting line-up included Robbie Keane and Damien Duff as the twin strikers, and it now seemed that, as far as the attacking department was concerned, McCarthy had made his mind up. The tiny terrors would almost certainly be unleashed on Cameroon in Ireland's opening World Cup encounter, with Niall Quinn providing a vastly experienced – and vastly alternative – option from the bench.

Their selection received the seal of approval from Taribo West, the Nigeria defender who had seen for himself how awkward it was to deal with Ireland's dynamic duo at Lansdowne Road.

'Up front Robbie Keane and Damien Duff are difficult to mark, as well as being creative,' he said after the game. 'Duff, particularly, is a big creator of chances as his movement takes him all across the front line.'

So Duff was odds-on to operate at centre-forward. The only concern with that, as Duff himself had already alluded to, was that his most effective work for the national side had seen him create chances for others rather than convert them himself. His goalscoring record for Ireland – one goal in twenty-six international appearances following the Nigeria game – was, in a word, disappointing.

In fairness, though, the stats didn't really tell the whole story. Nine of those twenty-six appearances had been as a substitute and, despite his recent conversion to a striker, most of his time as an international had been spent on the wing.

And he could clearly finish, judging by the five sometimes brilliantly executed strikes he plundered in his final ten Premiership outings of the 2001–2 campaign. As Duff had already pointed out to the press, that impressive goal return was a result of the considerable time he'd spent honing his predatory instincts on the Blackburn training ground under the watchful eye of Rovers' coach Dean Saunders.

'I think that Graeme [Souness] was quite happy to see Mick [McCarthy] use me as a centre-forward. He has often said to me that I could play there if I wanted to and the only thing he wants me to improve on is my shooting,' Duff told the *Evening Standard*.

'I have spent a lot of time getting in shooting practice with Dean Saunders and it has made a difference. I know when to shoot now and when to lay the ball off. That has helped me at Blackburn, even when I play on the wing, and it has definitely improved me as an international footballer. I think Dean has taught me elements of the striking role that I was only stumbling across without his input and that should stand me in good stead in the World Cup finals.'

As he and his Ireland teammates set off for Asia, Duff had every right to feel content. A fine campaign had seen him emerge as one of English football's most wanted players and he was about to fulfil a boyhood dream – of his own and every other aspiring young footballer – by spearheading his country's World Cup assault.

He had overcome the 'horrors' that had blighted his career not so long ago and, he felt, was a stronger character because of it. 'I'm definitely more able to cope now, with the Premiership and with international football,' he said. 'I'm more mature, more experienced and more able for anything that the game can throw at me. I have, if you like, served my apprenticeship and graduated now.

'I also have a better understanding of exactly what Mick wants me to do in Japan. I am looking forward to delivering for him now.'

Duff couldn't wait for the tournament to start, and neither could Ireland's jolly green army of fans. High hopes were pinned on a shy twenty-three-year-old starlet who was always keen to shun the spotlight and wasn't entirely comfortable with all the attention he was receiving. He needn't have worried: one of his colleagues was just about to take all the headlines in the most spectacular fashion.

CHAPTER 9

And It's Goodbye From Him...

'This is supposed to be the best experience of our
lives but the past couple of weeks haven't been nice.'

DAMIEN DUFF, MAY 2002

Roy Keane was, in some quarters, considered to be as instrumental to his team's chances of success at the 2002 World Cup as almost any other individual at the tournament. The captain and driving force of Mick McCarthy's side, he displayed an ability to excel in all areas of the pitch and inspire others around him, and this had been a fundamental feature of Manchester United's domestic domination and was now key to Ireland's hopes of progressing in the Far East.

'If McCarthy is to emulate Big Jack and take an entire nation on the emotional roller-coaster of a generation then Manchester United's Roy Keane must discover the defining moment of his career,' wrote Michael Scully in the *Mirror*, two weeks before the start of the World Cup.

'Keane is the one player in the Irish side who might trouble the selectors of a World XI. He is to the Irish cause what Zidane is to France, Figo to Portugal or Rivaldo to Brazil. Virtually irreplaceable.'

The role of the thirty-year-old midfielder in McCarthy's side had evolved from the one in which he operated under Jack Charlton. The direct, uncomplicated approach adopted by Charlton's team was a thing of the past. The 'new' Ireland game plan involved more passing, more pace, more trickery. Happily for Roy Keane, that meant more action.

'No disrespect to Jack Charlton, but now the midfield players actually get a touch of the ball,' Keane said in the *Sunday Express*. 'Under Jack it was no secret that he liked the long-ball game, getting it up the field early. I used to have a crick in my neck watching it fly by.'

The skipper was pleased with the change in playing style but, it would soon emerge, he was far from happy with a number of other issues regarding the Ireland setup. The problems that led to Keane's premature World Cup exit had been festering for some time before the infamous showdown with Mick McCarthy that proved to be his final act.

Having become accustomed to the very best treatment while representing Manchester United, Keane grew increasingly frustrated with the inadequate training facilities, travel arrangements and general preparation that, in his eyes, he and his teammates experienced when on international duty. He felt that the players should be treated with more respect by the Irish FA, and was irked by the easygoing, 'happy camper' attitude that seemed to be all too prevalent in the Irish camp.

By the time Keane joined up with Ireland's World Cup squad on the eve of their friendly meeting with Nigeria in Dublin, trouble was already brewing. Two days before the Nigeria game, Niall Quinn had been rewarded for sixteen years of international service with a testimonial match, between Ireland's World Cup team and his club side Sunderland, at the Stadium of Light.

Quinn received widespread acclaim for his decision to donate the entire proceeds of the game to hospitals in Dublin and Sunderland. Keane, too, was the subject of much press attention after the game, but not in a positive sense. He was a notable absentee at the Stadium of Light and, without knowing why, the media immediately cast Keane as the villain of the piece. 35,000 TURNED UP TO PAY TRIBUTE TO NIALL QUINN – ROY KEANE DIDN'T BOTHER, screamed a headline in Dublin's *Evening Herald*.

What didn't help the Irish captain's cause was the fact that, a few weeks earlier, he had refused to contribute to an article for the match programme because the piece was being written by Cathal Dervan, an Irish journalist disliked by Keane because he'd once urged the Lansdowne Road crowd to boo his every touch throughout an Ireland game.

Keane, it transpired, had not attended Quinn's match because he was feeling the strain of ongoing knee, hip and back injuries. The evening was his last at home before he was due to jet off to the World Cup, and he chose to spend the time with his wife and kids rather than sit in the stands at Sunderland.

He had informed the Ireland physio Mick Byrne of his decision before the game, but the reasons for his nonappearance were not immediately made public and a messy confusion followed. Consequently, Keane made a point of seeking out Quinn as soon as he arrived in Dublin for the Nigeria game – in which he did appear – to clear up the incident.

The matter was closed, but Keane was upset at the way the whole episode had been handled and wasn't in the best of moods as Ireland embarked on an arduous seventeen-hour flight to the Pacific island of Saipan, via Amsterdam and Tokyo.

Soon after arriving in Saipan, the players attended a welcoming barbecue to which journalists were also invited, forcing Keane to brush shoulders with those who had spent the previous week vilifying him for his Sunderland no-show. As you can imagine, the mood of the agitated skipper was hardly lightened by the experience.

Things weren't about to get much better. Mick McCarthy gathered the squad together for a meeting the night before training was due to start. There was a problem. The team's training equipment hadn't turned up – no footballs, no bibs, no medical equipment. It was another embarrassing incident for the Irish, and one that served only to stoke the simmering fire of discontent burning within Keane.

It was difficult for Keane, a man whose innate refusal to accept second best had long been his most prominent feature, to shrug his shoulders and dismiss the situation as being 'one of those things'. This was the World Cup, and he found it impossible to believe that the likes of Brazil, Argentina, Italy and Germany would ever encounter such problems.

An improvised training session was conducted on the Monday, and, even though the training gear finally arrived that evening, the state of the practice pitch was another cause for concern in Keane's opinion. The intense heat in Saipan had ensured a hard, dry surface that had not been watered ahead of Ireland's visit and was littered with potholes.

Keane was close to breaking point. Something had to give, and at the end of the second day's training it did. As the players prepared to finish the session with a short-sided game it was announced that the keepers would not be taking part. Shay Given, Dean Kiely and Alan Kelly had all started training half an hour before the rest of the squad and, goalkeeping coach Packie Bonner insisted, had worked hard enough already.

Keane was fuming: how could you have a game without keepers? After confronting Bonner as he left the field, he turned to Kelly, and a heated exchange ensued. Kelly told Keane he was too tired to participate and Keane snapped back, suggesting that his colleague wouldn't be too tired to play a round of golf the following day.

The skipper had had enough. Later that day he sat in the gardens of the team hotel with Mick McCarthy and informed the manager that he had made a decision. He wished to play no further part in Ireland's World Cup campaign. He was going home.

Cue bedlam. McCarthy accepted Keane's decision and made plans to replace his captain with Colin Healy, the young Celtic midfielder who had responded favourably when given a chance to impress during Ireland's pre-World Cup friendlies.

The situation was then put on hold as Keane announced that he was reconsidering his stance and a period of indecision followed. Finally, after seeking the opinions of those closest to him, including his wife Theresa and Manchester United manager Alex Ferguson, Keane made another announcement. He wasn't going anywhere, and was once again focused on leading Ireland's World Cup venture. With ten days to go before the opening game against Cameroon the captain was still on board – but only just.

Packie Bonner did his bit to try to play down the whole incident by telling the *Evening Standard*, 'Let me state quite clearly that I have had bigger rows with my son over his homework than I have had with Roy Keane this week. Yes, Roy and I did forcibly exchange opinions on Tuesday, but that was nothing more than a frank exchange of views on a World Cup training ground. It happens all the time in football, it was patched up that night and forgotten about the next morning.'

It seemed, on the surface, that the ship had been steadied. This, however, was merely the calm before an almighty storm.

It had already been a turbulent week for Mick McCarthy – who had seemingly lost his captain and most influential player on the Tuesday only to have him back in the fold on the Wednesday – by the time he was alerted of an article that had been published in Thursday's edition of the *Irish Times*.

The article in question involved an interview with Roy Keane that had been conducted the previous day. In it Keane explained how he had almost walked away from the World Cup, and spoke at length about the reasons for his discontent: the substandard training conditions, the travel arrangements, his treatment following the Sunderland match, the barbecue with the media, etc., etc.

Keane had been shown a copy of the article before it went to print by Tom Humphries, the journalist who had interviewed him, and had no qualms about its content.

McCarthy, on the other hand, did have a problem with it. He was unhappy with an article that he felt could cause unnecessary disharmony within the ranks. A now infamous team meeting was subsequently called and Keane was asked to explain his comments in front of his teammates.

What followed was, according to Niall Quinn's description of events in his autobiography, the 'most articulate, the most surgical slaughtering I've ever heard. Mick McCarthy is dismantled from A–Z – his personality, his play, his style, his tactics, his contribution... Roy is extraordinary when he gets going.'

Keane and McCarthy had never quite seen eye to eye, with their strained relationship dating back to the days when team captain McCarthy had attempted to instil some discipline into the impetuous international rookie Keane.

Now it was all coming out, as Keane launched a devastating personal assault on McCarthy. In his autobiography, Keane admits that part of his rant included, 'I didn't rate you as a player, I don't rate you as a manager and I don't rate you as a person.'

The players were stunned by Keane's ten-minute verbal volley. 'We came out of there like people who'd seen ghosts,' Quinn added.

McCarthy, visibly shaken by the whole affair, composed himself the best he could before announcing at a hastily arranged press conference that he was faced with no other option but to axe his captain from the squad.

'I cannot and will not tolerate being spoken to with that level of abuse being thrown at me, so I sent him home,' McCarthy said. 'I'm sad to lose him. As a player he's absolutely brilliant. He's one of the best in the world. But I have made the right decision not only for the benefit of me but for the squad. We will move on and be all right because we're collectively strong.'

The news sent shockwaves through the world of football and, thousands of miles away in Ireland, the whole saga engulfed a nation like never before. It was virtually impossible to find a member of the population who didn't have an opinion on the issue as every newspaper, TV and radio station devoted itself to the 'Keanegate' affair. Even Ireland's Prime Minister Bertie Ahern got involved.

Some sided with the manager and some with the banished skipper. Either way, it didn't look too good for Ireland. The World Cup would be challenging enough with Keane *in* the team, so how could the Irish public expect their boys to cope without their best player, their linchpin, their mercurial leader?

Maybe it wouldn't be so bad, though. Former Ireland striker Tony Cascarino, who appeared at two World Cups on his way to accumulating eighty-eight international caps, went as far as suggesting that Keane's departure would relieve the pressure on some of Ireland's younger players and could even act as a blessing in disguise.

Cascarino explained his thinking in his *Times* column, as he remembered how the absence of the suspended Keane had affected the team in a World Cup qualifier away to Estonia in the previous June. He wrote,

> I went to Tallinn for the Estonia game and it seemed like a weight had been lifted off some of the players' shoulders. They played with such freedom without the hollering and moaning from Roy, because he is so driven and desperate to win. But when it's not going right, he can get quite nasty and others will feel the sharp side of his tongue.
>
> I know some of the younger players feel uncomfortable in certain situations with Roy. Don't get me wrong, I played with Roy and know all about his ranting and raving, but that was an experienced Irish side and to the old pro it's water off a duck's back. This is a young Irish side and I feel a lot of them go into their shells when Roy starts having a go. Damien Duff is one and Matt Holland must find there's a lot of added pressure playing alongside Roy in midfield.

As the Keane debate reached fever pitch, there was still the small matter of some football to play. Ireland were leaving Saipan for Japan, where they would face J-League side Sanfrecce Hiroshima in what amounted to a final dress rehearsal before their World Cup opener. On the coach that took them from their Saipan hotel to the airport, a piece of paper was placed on the seat that Roy Keane usually occupied. 'RIP' had been scribbled on it by one of the players; clearly, not everyone was lamenting Keane's exit.

The meeting with Sanfrecce, one week before the Cameroon game, gave the players a much-needed opportunity to forget about you-know-who and concentrate once again on what they did best – playing football. With Duff partnering Robbie Keane up front and Mark Kinsella joining Matt Holland in a new-look central midfield pairing, Ireland won the match 2–1, but their joy was tempered by the sight of Jason McAteer being stretchered off with a knee injury.

After the game, rumours that Roy Keane could make a dramatic return to the team gathered pace. Striker David Connolly started the ball rolling by asking the most senior member of the playing squad, Niall Quinn, if there was a way of making it happen.

Quinn canvassed opinion among the players and the reaction was mixed, with some making it perfectly clear that Keane should not be allowed to return. One of those players, it's safe to say, was Matt Holland. Never noted for being outspoken, Holland was on this occasion stirred sufficiently to express publicly his dismay at Keane's behaviour.

'Keane lives in "Roy Keane World" and refuses to accept other people's autonomy or opinions," Holland wrote in his *Independent on Sunday* column. 'From the very start he moaned about, well everything really, and I feel, with the benefit of hindsight, that he wanted to go home all the time.'

As the days passed, talk of Keane's re-emerging in the Far East continued, but in the end it wasn't to be. A reconciliation proved out of the question and Ireland had a last-ditch attempt to call up Colin Healy as a replacement denied by FIFA because, they ruled, the circumstances under which Ireland had asked for special dispensation were not 'exceptional'.

One player who found the whole affair difficult to work out was Damien Duff. This was not what he expected the World Cup to be like, and Niall Quinn revealed Duff's despair when he said, 'He [Duff] was saying, "I watched [the World Cup in] Italy in 1990 and America four years later on the television and I always dreamed about playing in the World Cup. Is this it?"'

A couple of days before the big kick-off, Duff spoke to the assembled media about how his maiden World Cup adventure had been tarnished by the extraordinary events of the past week. 'It's not been nice for us young lads,' he said. 'This is supposed to be the best experience of our lives but the past couple of weeks haven't been nice with what's been going on.

'It's been a roller-coaster ride. It's been nonstop with something different happening every day, and it's not nice for us young lads at our first World Cup. Hopefully, it can be put to the back of everyone's mind and we can get on with it. In the past couple of days it's been out of everybody's mind, including the gaffer, so come Saturday we can do the business, hopefully.'

Having entered the tournament as one of Ireland's most talked-about players, Duff was certainly not complaining about being shunted from the limelight by Roy Keane's exploits. Besides, he was getting used to the pressure.

'I don't feel under any added pressure,' Duff continued. 'I

have been getting pressure all year at Blackburn. We had a relegation battle in the last couple of months. There was a lot of pressure there and I got through that, so hopefully I'll be able to do the business in the next few weeks.

'I've played left wing my whole life and that's where I'm most relaxed, so playing in the centre is all new to me. But, playing with the likes of Robbie Keane, Niall Quinn, Dave Connolly and Clinton Morrison every day, I'm only going to learn. I'm going to enjoy it and it's great to get out there. The most important thing is to get out of the group.'

Duff chose not to speak specifically about his departed skipper, and it wasn't until a couple of years later that he revealed the full extent of his adulation for Keane. Then, speaking to Ireland's *Sunday Independent* about the guidance Keane had offered him during the World Cup, Duff said, 'He took me under his wing, maybe a little bit. He pulled me aside the odd day to say a few words, but I can't say I was knocking up to his room for a bit of banter. I've the utmost respect for him, he's the greatest player I've ever played with. I love playing with him.'

While the Keane episode had dominated newspapers for several days, reporters still found space to keep alive what had become a popular news line of theirs. Duff was still being linked with a move away from Blackburn and, apparently, Inter Milan were now in the hunt for his signature.

'The speculation doesn't affect me at all,' Duff insisted. 'I haven't heard the rumour linking me with Inter, so it isn't going to bother me. I've been getting it for the past couple of months but I'm here now with the Republic squad, and when

I go back in July I shall be with Blackburn. I love it there and can't wait to get back, but first and foremost I can't wait to enjoy the World Cup.'

Whether the rumours were true or not, Brian Kerr, who had overseen the development of both Duff and Robbie Keane in their days as Ireland youth internationals, was quick to express his concerns – especially as Keane's San Siro switch had turned so sour in 2000.

'The Italian league is the best in the world but I don't reckon their squad system encourages young players' development,' Kerr said in the *Sunday Mirror*. 'Lads like Damien, and Robbie for that matter, need to be playing every week to flourish. Teams such as Inter have too many good footballers for anyone to be guaranteed a game every month, let alone every week!

'On the other hand, I've no doubt Duffer would be able to deal with the pressures of football at that level. He's very focused and committed. He loves his football and if Inter made a serious offer, I'd imagine he'd find it very hard to refuse. I'd just worry that he'd get lost in the system out there.'

CHAPTER 10

World Cup Wonders

'People speak highly of Michael Ballack, Luis Figo
and Rui Costa and do so partly because there is a mystique
about foreign players with great technical ability.
But Duff is in that class now.'

THE SUN, JUNE 2002

O n Saturday, 1 June, at long last, the 2002 World Cup
began in earnest for Ireland. A week described by
Mick McCarthy as 'the toughest of my life' was just about to
get a whole lot worse *or* take a decisive turn for the better.
Facing Ireland in Niigata's Big Swan stadium were
Cameroon, a strong, athletic side who had played England a
week earlier and only drawn 2–2 following Robbie Fowler's
last-gasp equaliser. The African and Olympic champions
were sure to provide a serious test.

Ireland had done their homework, though. McCarthy's
assistant, Ian Evans, had travelled to Mali earlier in the
year to watch Cameroon play in the African Nations Cup.
He felt that Winfried Schaefer's team would be vulnerable
to pacey strikers, and was confident that Ireland's nippy

forwards could exploit the considerable gaps that often existed between Cameroon's back three.

That assessment lent further support to the argument that Ireland's two starting strikers should be the fleet-footed Robbie Keane and Damien Duff, rather than the physically imposing Niall Quinn. Not that Mick McCarthy hadn't already decided on the starting composition of his forward line. That was obvious from comments he made before the game.

'I don't know anybody who would be happy to play against Robbie Keane and Damien Duff at the moment,' McCarthy told the press. 'They will cause problems for every team and they could be the stars of the World Cup if they don't get injured. Together they're a real threat to any defence.

'This is the first time for both of them in the World Cup finals. They both watched Irish teams of the past play in World Cup finals and were both desperate to come and play in them. They are two hungry young players who have got unbelievable ability, fabulous ability.

'Duffer has got pace, dribbling ability and tricks; Robbie complements him because he's quick in a different kind of way. He has quick feet and is a great finisher.

'If you watch them in training, you see they have a great understanding. If they get the protection that good players crave, then they could be sensational in this World Cup.'

Now it was time for action. The first rule of World Cup football – don't lose your opening game – was especially applicable this time round, as the loss of their leading man and the furore that followed meant that all eyes were on Ireland, eager to see how the team could cope. For a group of players who prided themselves on their great camaraderie and spirit, this was the ultimate test of their credentials.

The initial signs were not good. The heat was on for Ireland in more ways than one, and McCarthy's men struggled to deal with the sweltering conditions – and with their dominant opponents – in Niigata. The lively Samuel Eto'o wriggled free down the right to set up Patrick Mboma six minutes before half-time and, in turn, the powerful striker slipped the ball past Shay Given. Deadlock broken.

When the Ireland players returned to their dressing room at the break they could hardly complain about the 1–0 deficit. The manager had taken a well-publicised battering before the game and this was his chance to hit back. Now was the time for McCarthy to show his worth.

Someone had placed a sign on a dressing room board that read NO REGRETS. McCarthy pointed to those two words and told his players that, whatever happened in the next forty-five minutes, 'don't come back in here regretting what you could have done'. Changes had to be made in terms of application and personnel, so Jason McAteer, who was still feeling the effects of the knee injury he sustained a week earlier, was replaced by Steve Finnan.

Finnan slotted into his natural right-back position and shifted Gary Kelly up to right-midfield, as Robbie Keane and Duff – whose impact up to that point had been minimal – were told to neglect some of their defensive duties and play high up against the Cameroon back line in order to impose themselves on the game.

The turnaround was remarkable. With the second half

barely seven minutes old, Matt Holland pounced on a headed clearance to fire home from distance and level the scores with a priceless strike. Suddenly, a surge of belief shot through the side and transmitted itself into the watching masses of Irish fans draped in green, white and orange. At last, their World Cup had begun – and how they celebrated.

As the sun started to set, the heat was no longer an issue and Ireland continued to press. New skipper Steve Staunton and his central-defensive partner Gary Breen gradually got to grips with Mboma and Eto'o and the comeback was almost capped in perfect style when Robbie Keane's snapshot came back off a post.

Talk of the other Keane may have been banned by the manager but Ireland's vocal followers refused to oblige. 'Are you watching, Roy Keane?' they sang.

It stayed 1–1 and Ireland couldn't possibly be disappointed. They'd come through the most disruptive of build-ups and taken a point from a difficult game that, at the halfway stage, was fast slipping away from them.

Duff's performance had mirrored that of the team. He admitted after the game that the heat had made the going particularly tough in the first half, when he and fellow frontrunner Keane were starved of service and well shackled by the muscular Cameroon defence.

His work rate was first-class, though, and, as the game wore on, he became increasingly threatening and began to show exactly why he'd been tipped to shine at the tournament. It was a display that didn't go amiss in the following day's match reports.

At the front, Robbie Keane and Damien Duff were terriers against tigers, yet they toiled to construct a platform for their skills, and their character shone through their Godgiven talent.

– Mail on Sunday

Over the course of the 90 minutes Duff finished some way behind Matt Holland and Mark Kinsella in overall influence but he grew in stature as the game progressed. As it entered its final stages, Ireland were marauding, going for the jugular and Duff was comfortably the best player on the park.

– Sunday Times

True, people had earmarked the Blackburn playmaker as a potential star of the tournament, but it is much harder to deliver. He has done so now, with a creative and hard-working performance.

– Independent on Sunday

Another plus point for the Irish was the performance of Damien Duff up front.

With his constant movement into clever positions and ability to hold the ball up he ran [Rigobert] Song and [Raymond] Kalla ragged and they'll be glad to see the back of him.

– Sunday Mail (Scotland)

With people now talking about those members of the Ireland squad who were *at* the World Cup as opposed to the one who wasn't, there was a refreshing buzz about the players as they prepared for their second Group E encounter.

Germany, who dealt Saudi Arabia an 8–0 thrashing in their opening match, would provide the opposition, and it was a game that McCarthy's men approached with a quiet confidence.

Duff had once again been identified as Ireland's chief threat, initially by his Blackburn teammate Mark Hughes. The former Manchester United striker had been combining his playing duties at Ewood Park with the role of managing Wales, and, just a few weeks prior to the World Cup, Hughes's team beat Germany 1–0 in a Cardiff friendly with a goal from Rob Earnshaw.

The pace and movement of Earnshaw had caused Germany's sluggish defence no end of problems and Hughes predicted that Duff would have the same unsettling effect in Japan. 'Damien has all the attributes to do exactly what Earnshaw did for my team,' Hughes said to the *Sunday Mirror*. Germany's chief scout Uli Stielike was also aware of the menace posed by Duff. 'This guy is as fast as rocket' was his assessment in *The Times*.

Although they'd just hammered eight goals past Saudi Arabia, Germany were still not rated among the competition's most dangerous sides – it was only Saudi Arabia after all, reasoned the critics. But it wasn't quite the time to write off the Germans, as Ireland found out to their cost in Ibaraki, when Miroslav Klose added to the hat-trick he had plundered against the Saudis by heading past Shay Given to give Germany a nineteenth-minute lead.

Ireland were still trailing 1–0 as the half-time whistle sounded and, once again, a second-half comeback was required. Once again, McCarthy and his boys provided one and, once again, Duff was at the heart of it.

It looked as though the breakthrough had come ten minutes into the second period, when Kevin Kilbane rose to head Steve Finnan's cross into the path of Duff. But as the Rovers man fired goalwards from close range Germany goalkeeper Oliver Kahn extended his considerable frame to deflect the ball off-target with an exceptional save.

With time slipping away McCarthy threw on Niall Quinn to add his considerable weight to the attack while leaving both Keane and Duff on to forage for scraps off the big man.

The Quinn effect was immediate, as the substitute used his huge frame to cause havoc at the heart of Germany's startled defence. Ireland threw everything at Rudi Voller's men but still that vital goal eluded them. McCarthy and the rest of the Irish bench were on their feet. Thousands of supporters in emerald green frantically urged their team to score. Some couldn't bare to watch.

Then, with ninety-one minutes and forty-two seconds on the clock, Ireland equalised: a long punt forward, a majestic leap by Quinn and an emphatic finish by Keane. There was barely enough time for the goalscorer to execute his trademark celebratory cartwheel in front of Ireland's delirious fans before the final whistle went. If ever a draw felt like a victory, then this was it. 'The best Irish World Cup moment ever,' reckons Quinn.

Strains of 'You'll never beat the Irish' and 'There's only one Keano' (there was now, anyway) rang out around Ibaraki as Ireland celebrated as if they'd won the tournament.

Duff had constantly probed for a way to get his side back in the game and was again one of the night's outstanding performers. His post-match delight was blatantly evident. 'It's an unbelievable feeling, the best ever in my life,' he said. 'I thought it was gone, so to score in the last minute was unbelievable. I was looking at the clock through the last ten minutes and I thought that that was it. Then, to see it go in with virtually the last kick of the game... it just took an eternity to hit the back of the net.'

An experience that had started so gloomily for Ireland was now gaining momentum, and Duff was savouring every moment. 'This is a big step up from playing even the likes of Holland and Portugal,' he said in the *Sun*. 'This is the place to be. We've been playing against top-class players, especially in this game.

'I think we have done really well. It's so far, so good and let's see how it goes next Tuesday against Saudi Arabia. We always thought that we were more than capable of getting out of the group. Now we're on our way.

'I want to impress. That's all you ever want to do, especially now because we're on the biggest stage. I know I am more than capable of doing well and I want to prove that now. It's great to be here. I've done alright but I know I can do a lot better. I'm my biggest critic.'

Not just his biggest critic, but his only critic. That was how it appeared in an analysis of the media's reaction to the match.

The Daily Telegraph for one extolled his growing virtues: 'There are few sights more exciting than a player who takes on opponents. It is difficult to think of anyone at these finals so far who has done this more effectively than Duff against Germany. Every time he gained possession there was a buzz of expectancy and he rarely disappointed.'

The Sun proclaimed: 'In the last three months there has been a queue of players and former players waiting to tell us Damien Duff would take this tournament by storm. Well he has now, and after two games, you know that there is life after Roy Keane... There is a mystique about foreign players with great technical ability. But Duff is in that class now.'

A huge weight of expectancy had been placed on the shoulders of the red-hot Duff as he entered his first World Cup, and that pressure to perform had been intensified further by the departure of Roy Keane. The winger cum striker had been outstanding in the Premiership and torn several international defences apart in friendly matches, but some questions remained. Could he do it against the very best teams on the very biggest stage? In Ireland's first two games he had come up with all the right answers.

Someone else with plenty of questions to answer was Lynsey Duff, Damien's eighteen-year-old sister. She was at home in Ireland sitting her Leaving Certificate exam and, as a result, missed her big brother's second-half heroics against Germany. 'It is hard to focus when I know what's going on in Japan. I'll just have to keep my fingers crossed and watch the tape of the game later,' Lynsey told the *Mirror* as the game – and her exam – approached.

Three members of the Duff family who didn't miss a kick in Japan were Damien's parents Gerry and Mary and his thirteen-year-old brother Jamie. They had headed out East to monitor Ireland's progress at first hand – and the venture was fast turning into the trip of a lifetime.

Ireland now had a great chance of making it through to the last sixteen of the World Cup. Had Oliver Kahn kept out Robbie Keane's injury-time effort in Ibaraki – just as he'd managed to keep out everything else that the men in green had thrown at him – Ireland's faded qualification hopes would have rested in the hands of others. Now, they would decide their own fate.

The situation called for a celebration, and nobody in the Irish camp needed reminding of that. There would be no curfew, and the players were given strict instructions to have a few drinks, loosen up and savour the moment. In true Irish tradition, it would be a long, long night.

The New Otani hotel in the Tokyo suburb of Makuhari was the venue, and players, their families, officials, fans and journalists were all in attendance. They drank, they joked and, most of all, they sang. Some of the players opted for old classics, with Alan Kelly singing 'Suspicious Minds' and Richard Dunne – accompanied by his father – delivering a smooth rendition of 'Moon River'. Others went for tunes closer to their hearts, as Niall Quinn opted for the traditional Irish song 'Sliabh na mBan' and Robbie Keane sang 'Joxer Goes to Stuttgart', Christy Moore's celebration of Ireland's famous victory over England in 1988 (and a ditty that, some years later, Duff would select for a compilation CD of Chelsea players' favourite songs).

It was a real family affair for the Duffs. Gerry and Mary were celebrating their thirty-first wedding anniversary and at the heart of the festivities was young Jamie, impressing revellers with his guitar-playing ability. Not to be outdone, his older brother Damien belted out 'Bad, Bad Leroy Brown', a song that was written by Jim Croce and performed by Frank Sinatra but, on this occasion, belonged to Duffer.

Keane, Dunne and the Duff boys joined forces to sing 'Knocking on Heaven's Door' and those present couldn't help but be impressed with the whole event. Packie Bonner, along with the rest of the Irish public, had been aware of Damien Duff's footballing expertise for some time. Now he was wowing audiences with his vocal ability as well.

Talking to Scotland's *Sunday Mail*, Bonner wondered whether there was any limit to the boy's talents. He said, 'Apart from his ability as a footballer Damien Duff had us all stunned after the game last Wednesday with his singing ability. I'm telling you, the boy is a top chanter. He was up singing and it must have taken a lot for him to do that as he is such a shy young man. But Damien came out of his shell at the party when Mick allowed his lads to have a couple of beers and a right good sing-song.

'It got everyone going and we partied until 4 a.m. The fact that a guy with Duff's nature let himself go in front of a lot of people shows how comfortable everyone is with each other in the squad.'

A notable feature of Jack Charlton's stint as Ireland manager was the legendary manner in which each memorable success was celebrated, and Ireland's new wave of heroes were happy to continue that tradition in Tokyo. Mick McCarthy and his boys had conjured up a dramatic moment that would rank alongside the golden memories of Euro '88, Italia '90 and USA '94. No wonder they partied.

Niall Quinn had witnessed all those occasions and, as he basked in the New Otani hotel celebrations, he spoke of his joy at seeing Ireland's current crop of youngsters following in the footsteps of the players they had grown up idolising.

'This is a coming-of-age ceremony,' Quinn told the *Evening Standard*. 'I have always known that these kids singing here tonight can be better than any Irish team in the past. But the difference is that now they know it. When Robbie got that goal there was awe in the eyes of the Irish players dancing around him. They could not believe that one of their own had scored against one of the best soccer nations in the world. That goal and that result are priceless for Irish football.'

The next day saw Cameroon beat Saudi Arabia 1–0 to leave Ireland knowing exactly what they needed to do to make it into the knockout phase. Six days after drawing with Germany, McCarthy's men would have to beat Saudi Arabia by at least two goals in Yokohama to guarantee qualification (a one-goal victory would see their fate decided by the outcome of the Cameroon–Germany match).

In stark contrast to the murky atmosphere that had existed

on the eve of the tournament, there was now a relaxed, confident air about the Irish training base.

Several players had every right to be pleased with their contributions – Duff, according to the *Sunday Times*, more than anyone else: 'Though collectively Ireland have played well over the course of the two games, Duff has stood out comfortably as the team's best player.'

Following a Friday-afternoon training session, it was again Duff's turn to face the press. After he'd made himself comfortable – 'Mind if I sit down lads? Jaysus, I'm knackered!' – the interrogation of Ireland's Number 9 began.

He admitted that he didn't take the heat too well, that playing golf on rest days was 'too much work', that his loss of weight in recent years was certainly not the result of a particular fitness programme ('I don't even know what the Blackburn gym looks like') and that he'd spent every spare minute since arriving in the Far East in bed.

And, of course, he talked about the World Cup. 'This is definitely the biggest stage in the world,' he said. 'I came to this World Cup really wanting to impress. My philosophy is to leave here saying "no regrets". I don't want to be shy about expressing myself. I'm more than capable of holding my own among the best players in the world because I've always been confident in the ability I have.

'So far I've been happy with the way I have played. I'm not bothered about the attention of defenders. If two or three are chasing me, that's fine. I'm used to it.

'If you give everything you have, then you know in your heart you couldn't have done any more and that's the way we all seem to be playing right now. I've done OK at this World Cup so far but I know I can do a lot better. I'm my own biggest critic so I won't settle for second best.'

It was not only at international level that Duff was flourishing. He had become one of the Premiership's most dangerous attackers after developing a consistency that had long eluded him. For that, Duff was ready to acknowledge, Graeme Souness deserved great credit. 'The manager at Blackburn is always on at young players like myself and Matt Jansen to play to our ability and fulfil our potential,' he said.

'It's important to him that we develop and learn good habits and he encourages us to play. He dropped me the season before last. He told me, "With your ability, we need to get more out of you." Since then he's been on my back pushing me and I think that has carried me on to the international stage. Remember, just twelve months ago I wasn't even a regular in the Irish side. It's been a hell of a year.'

Duff's appreciation of the Rovers boss probably influenced his response when he was quizzed on the familiar subject of his future at club level. 'I read the papers before I came away and I saw my name linked with some pretty big clubs, but I'm happy at Blackburn,' he said. 'The attraction of playing for a bigger club sometime would appeal to me, because everyone wants to play in the Champions League. Blackburn are a big club, but the Champions League is the place to be. Having said that, Blackburn are in Europe next season and, although it's not the Champions League, I will relish the challenge.'

As the Saudi Arabia game drew closer Mick McCarthy could afford himself a wry smile. It was, after all, his substitutions that had prompted an upturn in fortunes for Ireland against both Cameroon and Germany. Judging by the reaction to the positive outcome on each occasion, McCarthy had, in his own words, evolved from 'a complete buffoon to a tactical genius' if football's fickle followers were to be believed. 'Bloody marvellous' he grinned.

It was a case of 'so far so good' for Ireland and their manager, but there were still suggestions that McCarthy should tinker with his line-up. Niall Quinn had posed such a useful threat during his cameo appearance against the Germans that the clamour for him to be handed a starting place alongside Keane – with Duff reverting to his natural position on the left wing – was increasing.

The idea was put to McCarthy but his stance was adamant. In his opinion, using Quinn from the bench represented one of his team's most potent weapons. 'When I was playing and you'd been going for some seventy minutes, the last thing you wanted to see was a six-foot-four guy warming up on the touchline,' said the former centre-half. Point made.

But Ireland had to go for goals, and if there was a concern it was that, despite his obvious threat, their Number 9 had gone ten months since his one and only international strike. Duff was fully aware of the situation.

'I've played left-wing since I was nine or ten and obviously I understand it more,' he said. 'But ever since the Portugal game [the World Cup qualifier in June 2001] Mick has played me up front. It's a lot different and there's pressure on you to score goals, which I haven't done yet, but I do enjoy it and I love playing with Robbie.'

Matchday brought the shops and offices of Dublin to a standstill, as pubs and bars filled to capacity. Others opted to watch from the comfort of the homes they had lovingly decked out in green, white and orange.

Hospitals in Ireland, meanwhile, were on red alert. Dr Chris Luke, a consultant in the accident and emergency unit of Cork's University Hospital, explained to the Press Association, 'After the first game against Cameroon, there was a steady trickle of patients who had injured themselves by jumping up and down in front of the TV. Young men sustained ankle strains and people jabbed themselves in the eye with glass tumblers. One woman sustained a very severe laceration by jumping up and landing on a vase in her sitting room.'

Inside the magnificent Yokohama stadium, spectators had barely taken their seats by the time Robbie Keane fired Ireland into an early lead, as the Leeds striker continued exactly where he had left off against Germany.

Instead of building on that early breakthrough, Ireland seemed to sit back, unfamiliar with the concept of being in front having conceded the first goal in each of their previous two games. A scrappy first half ended with Shay Given being called into action to preserve what was increasingly looking like a fragile lead.

Ireland needed some sort of fresh impetus, so McCarthy hauled off Ian Harte, threw on Niall Quinn and told Duff to attack the opposition from the left wing.

Just as his substitutions had done in the first two games,

McCarthy's switch paid dividends. Quinn beefed up an attack that had been dealt some pretty rough treatment in the opening period and Duff, given the freedom of the flank, was simply mesmeric.

Gary Breen doubled Ireland's lead to give them the two-goal advantage that was necessary for qualification and, with three minutes remaining, the moment Damien Duff had been longing for finally arrived.

Having latched onto Matt Holland's pass, Duff composed himself before unleashing an angled left-footed drive towards goal. Saudi keeper Mohammed Al-Deayea was perfectly placed to repel the effort but, sadly for him, his handling ability was clearly no match for his positioning skills. His fumbled attempt at a save served only to take the sting out of the ball on its way into the net.

Duff celebrated in style, facing the crowd and executing a Japanese bow of gratitude that, he has since joked, he'd been 'practising in front of the bathroom mirror all week'. The locals – not to mention the Irish supporters – were delighted with the routine.

It wasn't a classic strike by any means, but Duff couldn't care less. At twenty-three years of age he was a World Cup goalscorer and his team, 3–0 winners, had claimed a place in the last sixteen. It was the perfect way to cap another brilliant display from Duff and, continuing a trend, he was showered with plaudits after the game.

'Damien's second-half performance was up there with any display I have ever seen an Irish player give,' Quinn said in the *Sun*. 'That includes the great days of Liam Brady and

Johnny Giles, which I saw. Anyone you want, Paul McGrath or whoever. Duffer is a phenomenon and there appears to be no limit to what he can do. The goal will do him the world of good because I know he feels a little under pressure to deliver the goods.'

It appeared as though nothing was beyond this wispy winger-turned-striker-turned-winger-again. He could even look into the future, judging by his post-match comments.

'I had a feeling in the past week, even months, that I was going to score in this game so I'm glad it went in,' Duff told the assembled press. 'I had a premonition or something like that. It was very lucky but I'm very happy with it. Isn't it every young fella's dream to play in a World Cup and to score? I've done that but most important was for all the lads in the team to get through. We've done that and we're all really happy.'

Duff insisted that the overphysical attention he received in the first half didn't bother him, and also looked ahead to the second round. 'I was getting kicked, but that's as per usual: I'm used to getting that every Saturday throughout the season,' he said. 'I enjoyed it on the left. I had a lot more space and saw a lot more of the ball. It's the position I'm most used to and it probably showed.

'We're ready for the next round. We have done very well against two world-class teams already in Cameroon and Germany, so we're not going to fear Spain, if that's who we're playing. We can play a lot better, everybody knows, but the most important thing was to get through.'

Ireland fans everywhere partied long into the night. Back

home, ecstatic supporters spilled out of pubs and bars and onto the streets. In Japan everyone got 'Yokohammered' according to the *Sun*. Mick McCarthy spoke of his ambition to win the World Cup and Bertie Ahern said he couldn't wait for the next game. Just another day in Ireland's wacky World Cup adventure.

As Duff had predicted, Ireland's second-round opponents were Spain. José Antonio Camacho's team had beaten Slovenia, Paraguay and South Africa in the opening phase and only Brazil could match their 100 per cent group record. As ever, the Spanish outfit was packed with players of supreme technical adeptness, but, after a series of big-tournament disappointments, there were still question marks over their ability to excel when the stakes were raised.

The whole competition had just kept getting better and better for Ireland. They were now one game away from emulating the boys of Italia '90 by reaching the World Cup quarter-finals, and Mick McCarthy was being hailed a hero.

Back in the northwest of England, Blackburn Rovers officials were bracing themselves for the flurry of transfer bids that were reportedly imminent. The list of clubs interested in prising Duff away from Ewood Park was extensive enough *before* his World Cup exploits. Now he was even hotter property. 'We hope to start talking about new terms when he gets back,' John Williams, the Blackburn chief executive, told *The Times*.

McCarthy's concern regarding Duff was much more immediate. A sore knee forced him to miss training, and, while the manager insisted that it was purely a precautionary measure, reporters speculated that Ireland may have to face Spain without their most incisive offensive threat.

They needn't have worried, as Ireland started the game in the South Korean city of Suwon with an unchanged line-up. What followed was another unforgettable, emotional, action-packed evening of high drama. This time, though, there was to be no happy ending for the Irish.

For the third time in four games, Ireland found themselves 1–0 down when Fernando Morientes expertly steered a header beyond Shay Given after just eight minutes. But the magnificent spirit that Ireland had shown throughout the tournament meant that a comeback was almost inevitable.

The introduction of Quinn after fifty-four minutes, as a replacement for Gary Kelly, saw Duff move out to the right wing. He immediately slotted into his third position of the World Cup and within moments had tempted Spain defender Juanfran into a foul inside the box and Ireland were awarded a penalty. Ian Harte took responsibility from the spot but his weak effort was saved by Iker Casillas and Kevin Kilbane made a complete mess of the rebound.

With Duff and Keane probing from all angles and Quinn's presence causing its usual nuisance, Ireland's assault was unrelenting. In the last minute they were rewarded for their persistence when Fernando Hierro's desperately heavy-handed attempts to quell the threat of Quinn resulted in another spot kick. This time the ice-cool Robbie Keane made no mistake.

Not only did Ireland go into 'golden goal' extra time with

the momentum of that late equaliser, but they also had the advantage of playing against ten men after Spain's David Albelda limped out of the action with his team having already made their three allotted substitutions.

It was an advantage they failed to press home, however, and, if Ireland were to claim a quarter-final place, they would have to replicate the manner in which the team of Italia '90 did so – via a penalty shootout.

Sadly, it proved beyond them. Keane and Steve Finnan both converted their efforts but Matt Holland rattled the crossbar while Kilbane and David Connolly were denied by Casillas. Duff remained in the centre circle after opting not to offer his services. 'My one great regret,' he would later admit. Gaizka Mendieta stroked home a fortuitous winner that bobbled over Shay Given, and Ireland's World Cup excursion was over.

A glorious run had come to an end in the most agonising fashion. Irish players and supporters applauded each other in a touching display of mutual appreciation as both fought to stem the flow of tears.

There was plenty more appreciation in the days that followed. 'For me, the star player was Damien Duff. He's had some great moments,' said Jack Charlton in the *Mirror*. 'It was Duff's change of position that offered them inspiration,' according to *The Times*. 'Unusually, he was anchored to the right wing, rather than the left but the freedom he now found to work in still caused carnage.'

In the *Irish Times* Mark Lawrenson wrote, 'It was a wonderful team effort but I have to pay special tribute to

Damien Duff. I thought he was absolutely supreme. He took on defenders on the inside, the outside, on the right, and the left, showing great balance and pace. He has excelled on the world stage.'

It wasn't quite over for Ireland. Two days after the Spain defeat they arrived home in Dublin for a Tuesday-night reception in Phoenix Park. The response was incredible. An estimated crowd of one hundred thousand turned out to welcome home their heroes, as Westlife kicked off proceedings before the onstage arrival of Mick McCarthy and his boys was greeted with a deafening roar.

The biggest cheers were reserved for Damien Duff and Robbie Keane, with Duff taking the microphone to thank the adoring masses: 'Whether you are in Japan or Korea or back home here, you are the best fans in the world. Thank you very much.'

This was no ordinary welcome-home party. But, then again, it had been no ordinary summer for the people of Ireland.

CHAPTER 11

A Wanted Man

'I would not blame clubs for making offers.
He's a very good player.'
GRAEME SOUNESS, JULY 2002

Nothing quite enhances a footballer's stock like starring at the World Cup. All of a sudden they're catapulted to a level of stardom as yet uncharted, with the public gaze tracking their every move. Damien Duff was now a global star, and everything had gone a bit bonkers.

Talk of a move away from Blackburn Rovers was nothing new. That had been going on, intermittently, for a number of years, and had reached a frenzied state after Duff's sensational finish to the previous season had eased Rovers away from the drop zone. All approaches, however, were rebuffed.

Prior to the World Cup, Blackburn's most prized asset had spoken favourably of his genteel life in the northwest of England. A private man from an extremely tight family unit – 'every night I call my mam and dad up' – he was clearly settled in the peaceful surroundings of Lancashire's Ribble

Valley. Living 'up in the mountains' in a modest three-bedroom place that often housed visiting family and friends, he numbered among his spare-time activities sleeping, snooker and a spot of golf in nearby Clitheroe. He was in no rush to get away.

'I live on my own,' he told the *Irish Times*. 'I call around to the lads or they call around to me. The Ma and Da are over all the time. I've been good friends with Ally Mahon, Lucas Neil, an Australian, and a couple of young Irish fellas in the reserve team, but I've been four years there, living on me own. I'm used to my own space now. The family come and go. The lads come and go. My mates from Dublin, they come and go. I live for football, though. That sounds weird, but I get up every day and I'm dying to go in for training. The rest of the time I just sleep and eat.'

Whispers of a transfer escalated wildly after the World Cup. Duff had been one of the tournament's most exciting performers, and, while Blackburn were unable to offer him Champions League football or even a genuine title challenge, plenty of clubs in a position to provide both were intent on luring Duff away from Ewood Park.

Duff, who had two years remaining on his Rovers contract, remained committed to the Blackburn cause, judging by comments he made in the *News of the World* at the end of June 2002. 'This club has a great tradition in English football,' he said of the only professional outfit he had ever represented. 'And I'm confident that with decent luck, the good times are on the way back to Ewood Park. Blackburn is the only club I've known since coming to

England. And, all things being equal, that's where I want to stay.

'People say that you've a better chance when you're with one of the bigger outfits. But I did all right in the World Cup on the back of my season at Ewood Park, and I'm happy enough to stay. Who knows what will happen in the future? But for the present, I'm content to remain at the club and happy to be among so many friends.'

Although a string of potential suitors had been mooted, the list of runners racing for Duff's signature was soon whittled down to two main contenders. Duff's contentment in the northwest was well known, so it was no real surprise that Liverpool and Manchester United were the clubs vying for pole position in one of the summer's hottest transfer chases. For a player who was clearly at ease in Lancashire, the advantage of joining a leading European club without having to find a new home was obvious.

Both Liverpool and Manchester United remained tight-lipped, although Alex Ferguson did hint in a press conference that Duff's excellent World Cup showing had done his club's pursuit of a player whose price tag had now soared no favours at all.

'We haven't drawn up a big list of potential targets,' Ferguson said of United's summer transfer policy. 'You don't do that when you're trying to achieve what we are trying to achieve. With the quality and type of player we want to bring to the club you only have a list of four or five players who are operating at the highest level, and you feel could enhance the team. The World Cup beat us, though, because two or three players emerged over there who we had made enquiries for before it started.'

While Liverpool, United and Blackburn continued to haggle over Ireland's latest star, two of the nation's former World Cup heroes lent their weight to the debate over Duff's future. John Aldridge and Kevin Moran were both forthcoming with advice on the issue, both suggesting the direction in which they felt his career path should turn. Their views were none too surprising.

'I've been raving about Duff for the last five months,' said ex-Anfield legend Aldridge, in the *Mirror*. 'Liverpool should go for him now even though he's doubled in price after the World Cup. He's been the star of the tournament and he'll end up playing for one of the best clubs in the world now because he'll leave Blackburn, I'm convinced of that.'

Moran, who had been a fearless centre-half for Ireland, Manchester United and Blackburn, was sure of the best move for everyone concerned. For him, it had to be United.

'Duffer would handle the Old Trafford stage without any problems whatsoever,' he said in the *Manchester Evening News*. 'He'd have no trouble taking that on board and the fans at United would absolutely love him. United supporters love the kind of a player he is. They like players who can excite them and when Damien Duff gets going he can excite.

'Damien's got that unique ability to go by people for fun. He can do it either way. The great thing about Damien is that he's not predictable. Defenders don't know whether he'll take them on the inside or the outside so they are always in two minds and on the back foot. He can also score goals with both feet as well so he has a lot going for him. Another of his assets is that he's still improving.'

Blackburn responded to the situation by putting together a new deal for Duff – whose own response had been to take a much-needed holiday – that would help persuade him to remain a Rover.

'It is the club's intention to negotiate an extension to Damien's contract at the earliest opportunity,' Blackburn chief executive John Williams informed the press.

'Clearly, everyone at the club would like Damien to stay. But it's essential he signs the new contract on offer. We need to protect our assets and talks with him will begin as soon as he returns. I've spoken with the manager Graeme Souness and he's confident he can persuade Damien to remain with us on football grounds, at least for the foreseeable future.'

Souness, who was himself in the middle of new contract negotiations, had overseen Duff's development into one of the Premiership's most lethal weapons, and he knew that enticing a replacement of equal quality to Blackburn would be extremely difficult. If Rovers were to build on their commendable finish to the previous campaign and make a notable impact in the UEFA Cup, Souness needed to keep hold of his leading men. And it wasn't just Duff's growing influence *on* the pitch that had impressed his boss.

'Before, you wouldn't have even known he was in our dressing room,' Souness said in an interview with the *Sunday Express*. 'He had nothing to say for himself. Now in every way he is more confident instead of just being a boy. If he has something to offer he is not afraid to say so.

'By the end of this season he will prove himself as one of the biggest players in the league. He has always been one of those players you don't want to lose. I'm about to sign my own new four-year contract and I want players like Damien to remain here. This is a proper football club without egos.'

But before long Souness had given hope to all interested parties by claiming that Blackburn *would* be prepared to part with Duff if they received a substantial offer for their star man.

'If someone like Internazionale came along with an offer of ridiculous money then we'd have to consider it,' he said. 'I've been in the game long enough to know how simple economics work. The fact remains we have not had any offers for Damien and we don't want any either because, at this moment in time, he's not for sale.'

If going public with such comments was a ploy by Souness to trigger a response then it worked. The following day the Rovers boss admitted that Liverpool had made a call to Blackburn, asking if Duff was available. 'The answer was "no",' he said, before effectively challenging those interested by adding, 'But if the price was right we would not be in a position to turn a ridiculous offer down.'

That price had escalated, Souness argued, following Rio Ferdinand's switch from Leeds to Manchester United for a fee somewhere in the region of £30 million. If that was the going rate for a defender, then what price a goalscoring winger?

'It is going to take twenty-million-plus,' Souness told Sky Sports News, shortly after Blackburn had received a second enquiry regarding the player. 'If Rio Ferdinand is worth that money [£30m] then it must be the same for Duff. Traditionally, strikers who make and take goals bring in more money so maybe he [Duff] is worth more money.

'I would not blame clubs for making offers. He's a very good player.'

The game of cat-and-mouse continued, with Blackburn attempting to appease their own fans by claiming that selling Duff was the last thing they wanted to do, while at the same time sending out a 'make-us-an-offer-we-can't-refuse' message to Liverpool and, almost certainly, Manchester United.

'We have not had a bid for Damien Duff and we've made it quite clear that we would not encourage one,' said John Williams in *The Times*, on the eve of Blackburn's opening game of the Premiership season against Sunderland. 'If we had received a £10m bid, it would have been turned down flat. The fact that there has been interest in Damien this summer is an open secret and we have had inquiries from two clubs, of which Liverpool are one. But we have consistently made it clear that we don't wish to sell him.'

The saga had dragged on for several weeks and so it was with much relief that Rovers fans watched Duff kick off the new season in the blue and white of Blackburn, even though he'd yet to sign the new deal on offer at Ewood Park. With the transfer deadline approaching, Liverpool finally made a firm bid to prise their top target away from Blackburn. Rovers' response was swift.

'Liverpool made a bid for Damien Duff after weeks of speculation but it was nowhere near good enough,' said Souness. 'It wasn't even half of what we wanted. It took ten seconds for our chief executive John Williams to send back a fax. There had been talk of offers but there had not been one until last week and that is the 100 per cent truth.'

At the end of August, after none of the chasing clubs had been able to provide an offer that matched Blackburn's valuation of the player, Duff put pen to paper on a new deal at Blackburn, extending his contract by two years to keep him at Ewood Park – in theory – until 2006. The new terms, it would later emerge, included a release clause that would allow Duff permission to talk to another club in the future if that club offered a particular amount of money for his services (a figure that was undisclosed at the time).

Most newspaper reports estimated that the improved terms would earn Duff around £30,000 a week. The *Daily Telegraph* went even further, suggesting, 'Damien Duff was last night set to become the best-paid player in Blackburn's history, earning around £40,000 a week under the terms of a new contract.'

Duff was just glad that the whole episode, and the considerable attention it had created, had finally been brought to a conclusion. 'I've proved my commitment by signing,' he said in the *Express*. 'The last couple of months have been unsettling, especially when you consider how much I enjoy where I am playing. But it's a relief to finally get it out of the way by signing the deal. Now I just want to put it all behind me and concentrate on playing because we had a good season last year and I know we can do better. I have been at Blackburn since I was 16. I love it here and I was happy to sign the new deal.'

Duff later revealed that the arrival of Dwight Yorke at

Ewood Park had helped sway his decision to stay with the club. Yorke had been signed from Manchester United, and the prospect of seeing him reform the devastating strike partnership with Andy Cole that had plundered so many goals at Old Trafford was too good to resist.

'It was flattering to be linked to some big clubs,' Duff said in the *Sun*. 'But the priority was to improve and, as far am I am concerned, the best place for me to do that is at Blackburn. Last season was a big year for me. It went well but I know myself that I have a lot more to learn. I have done nothing as a player yet.'

And, with the World Cup now behind him, Duff knew that it was time to create some new glories rather than live off past ones.

'When I look back on the World Cup now, I am definitely happy with how it went for me. Last season was a big year for me and, thankfully, it went well but there is still more for me to learn.'

As a man who'd never made secret the fact that all he ever wanted to do was play football, Damien Duff couldn't wait for the 2002–3 season to get going.

Out on the football pitch was where he felt most comfortable, not in the transfer gossip columns of national newspapers, and expressing himself with a ball at his feet in front of thousands of spectators always felt more natural than addressing a small gaggle of reporters. The chance to lace his boots up and start terrorising opposing defenders once again couldn't come quickly enough.

Unfortunately for Duff, an injury setback was never too far away, and the first of several niggles that would interrupt his season flared up at the beginning of September.

Having enjoyed a routine 3–0 friendly win away to Finland in their first post-World Cup outing the previous month, Ireland travelled to Moscow to face Russia in their opening fixture of the Euro 2004 qualifying campaign. In contrast to Ireland, Russia had endured a miserable 2002 World Cup, with furious fans rioting in Moscow following a 1–0 defeat to Japan that eventually contributed to their group-stage exit. Ireland, on the other hand, had seen their standing enhanced in the wake of the World Cup, and were fancied to claim a favourable result from what was traditionally a tricky-looking trip to Eastern Europe.

With Switzerland, Albania and Georgia making up Group 10, Ireland were the section's top seeds, and Irish fans were expecting nothing short of qualification for their team's first European Championships finals since 1988.

Russia, though, had a new manager to impress and a smarting nation to appease. They scored twice within the space of five first-half minutes to establish an advantage and refused to relinquish their lead. The final 4–2 scoreline dealt Mick McCarthy the heaviest defeat of his Ireland reign, and those endless nights of celebration in the Far East suddenly seemed a long, long time ago.

Duff's night lasted just eighteen minutes before a thigh injury forced him out of the action. For a player not unfamiliar with muscular injuries, the exertions of a demanding few months appeared to have taken their toll.

'Something has been coming for the last couple of weeks because my legs have felt tired,' Duff said in *The Times*. 'I suppose all the travelling and everything else has caught up with me.'

Graeme Souness, meanwhile, was not in such a philosophical mood. In fact, the Blackburn boss was fuming. 'I think they [the Irish FA] should be paying compensation,' he told the *Sun*. 'These players are real assets. Damien has signed a very lucrative new contract with us. If I ran an engineering company with a factory full of expensive machines and someone said "I want your best machine for a week", and it came back broken, I'd expect compensation. What other business is there where you wouldn't be compensated? Why should football be any different? It's frustrating.'

The Irish FA confirmed that Blackburn would be 'adequately compensated' for the breakdown of their best machine, but barely six weeks later there was another spanner in the works.

Ireland were beaten 2–1 by Switzerland at Lansdowne Road to leave their chances of Euro 2004 qualification – and, all of a sudden, the position of Mick McCarthy – under serious threat. Duff appeared for eighty-two minutes of the match before being withdrawn, and subsequently returned to his club with a strained hamstring.

While Souness was shaking his head in disbelief, the consequences of his latest niggle were potentially heartbreaking for Duff. In the UEFA Cup, Blackburn had been drawn to face one of the teams Duff had followed since boyhood, Celtic, and he was on the brink of fulfilling a lifelong dream by running out at a packed Parkhead – if he could get himself fit in time.

Rovers had booked themselves into the second round of the competition following an eventful opening tie against CSKA Sofia. A 1–1 draw at Ewood Park in the first leg was not the best of results, but, by the time Duff had fired Blackburn into a 3–0 lead after fifty-eight minutes of the return meeting, it appeared to be game, set and match to the visitors.

Duff's strike, his first in European competition, was an angled drive that silenced the partisan crowd in the Bulgarian capital and left the home side needing an improbable four goals to emerge victorious. They got three of them but, dramatically, Rovers held on to progress via the away-goals rule, clinching a place in the second round of the UEFA Cup for the first time in the club's history.

In Duff's eyes, Blackburn couldn't have wished for a more exciting second-round draw. Ironically, he had turned up for training one day at Blackburn earlier that year wearing a Celtic shirt – a brave move, considering his manager's past association with Glasgow Rangers. The story goes that when the Bhoys fan returned to the changing rooms after the session his beloved green and white jersey had mysteriously vanished.

Duff was overjoyed with the draw. 'Personally, I think it's brilliant,' he said in the *Mirror*. 'This is a boyhood dream for me and for many of the Irish lads here [at Blackburn]. When I heard the draw I was over the moon. We were just out playing head tennis when a couple of the lads shouted it out and I thought they were winding me up at first. But it's a great draw and everyone's buzzing about it. I've followed Celtic from the moment I got into football, as every young Irish lad does.'

As the first leg trip to Glasgow edged nearer Duff fought desperately to get fit. 'Celtic have always been a bit special for me, but at this point I don't know whether I'll be fit to play against them,' he told the *News of the World*. 'But it does give me an extra reason to get back into full training at the earliest possible date. From the moment I was injured it was always in my mind to try to get back for this game.'

In other reports Duff revealed himself to be a big fan of the player most likely to threaten Blackburn's chances of progression in Europe, Henrik Larsson. The Swedish striker's tally for the season already stood at eighteen goals by the time Rovers arrived in Glasgow at the end of October, so it was no surprise that Duff identified him as the hosts' chief danger man.

'Henrik is the man we must watch,' he said. 'I bought a Larsson shirt for an Old Firm game last season – it was just for the craic. What he's done for Celtic is unbelievable.'

The good news for Blackburn was that Duff regained fitness in time to start both legs. The bad news was that no one seemed to have taken much notice of his pre-match warning about Celtic's most lethal weapon. Larsson scored the only goal of the first match and added another in a 2–0 win at Ewood Park as Celtic dumped Rovers out of Europe and emerged triumphant from what the media had dubbed 'The Battle of Britain' (as is customary when English teams face Scottish teams in European competition).

By the turn of the year, Blackburn were sitting comfortably in the mid-table zone of the Premiership and were still in with a shout of repeating their heroics of the previous season by retaining the League Cup. Walsall (on penalties), Rotherham (via a 4–0 win in which Duff was among the scorers) and Wigan (2–0) were all dispatched before Rovers earned an impressive 1–1 draw away to Manchester United in the first leg of the semi-final.

That result meant the tie was perfectly poised when United made the short trip north for the return match two weeks later. It proved to be a most fruitful journey for the visitors. On another frustrating evening for Duff, he lasted just thirty-four minutes before yet another hamstring problem brought his night's work to a premature end. United completed a 4–2 aggregate victory. The League Cup trophy was on its way out of Ewood Park and Duff was back on the sidelines.

Anyone who thought that the Roy Keane saga had been buried in the past following Ireland's memorable World Cup display was badly mistaken. The team had made a disastrous start to their Euro 2004 qualifying campaign, losing their opening two games, and the growing band of supporters rallying for a Keane return were hardly helping Mick McCarthy's cause.

The problem was, McCarthy and his former captain were no closer to making up than they had been in Saipan. The Ireland squad clearly wasn't big enough for the two of them.

In November 2002, less than five months after taking his country to within a penalty shootout of the World Cup quarter-finals, McCarthy ended his reign of almost seven years by resigning as Ireland boss. 'Some of the negativity directed at me was affecting the players,' he said.

For Duff, it signalled the exit of his only ever senior international manager, the man who'd handed him his first cap as a nineteen-year-old fledgling back in 1998, and had overseen his development into one of the national team's most influential players.

The ensuing question of who should replace McCarthy threw up a whole host of interesting names. Bryan Robson was heavily linked to the vacancy, and was favoured by those who were hoping that his considerable standing at Old Trafford would help tempt Roy Keane back into the international fold.

Other names in the mix included John Aldridge, Peter Reid and Japan's World Cup boss Philippe Troussier. None of the aforementioned were given the job, though. The man who was eventually named as McCarthy's successor was Dubliner Brian Kerr, and that was good news for Damien Duff.

Kerr, who was virtually unknown outside his home country, had made his name by masterminding the most successful spell ever in the history of Ireland's youth teams. In 1998 he led both the Under-16s and Under-18s to success in their respective European Championships, with future senior internationals John O'Shea, Liam Miller, Andy Reid, Robbie Keane, Richard Dunne and Gary Doherty all starring for him that summer.

Duff missed that Under-18s success of 1998 because of a hernia operation, but he was one of the outstanding players on show when Kerr's Ireland side finished third at the 1997 World Under-20s Championship in Malaysia, and also played under him in the same competition two years later. Kerr knew the Blackburn man almost as well as anyone, and Duff gave the new appointment a big thumbs-up.

'Brian took me to Malaysia even though I was a couple of years younger than some of the lads and I've never forgotten that,' he said in the *News of the World*. 'That was a big vote of faith in me but he motivated the squad so well that I never really felt out of place. I'm looking forward to meeting up with him again.'

Injury forced Duff to miss Kerr's opening game, a 2–0 win in Scotland, but he was back to lead the forward line in the new manager's first competitive challenge, away to Georgia at the end of March. It was the third match of Ireland's quest for a Euro 2004 place, and losing again – as they had done against Russia and Switzerland – was simply not an option.

Thanks to two players already familiar with the ways of the new man in charge, Ireland didn't lose. Better than that, they came away with a victory after a frightening experience in Tbilisi that saw crazed home fans shower the opposition with coins, ball bearings and bottles, while Kevin Kilbane was struck with an open penknife.

Duff opened the scoring in the first half when he claimed a rare 'scruffy' goal, pouncing to force home the loose ball after Lee Carsley's shot had come back off a post. It was a poacher's strike, the type of which had not always been evident in Duff's repertoire, but it was a welcome addition to the mostly spectacular collection of goals he had claimed up to that point.

After Georgia had drawn level Duff was heavily involved again, providing the late cross from which Gary Doherty eventually scored the winning goal.

'It wasn't the prettiest of goals but they all count,' Duff said of his strike afterwards. 'It's a great result for Brian and for Ireland. The only thing that mattered coming out here this week was an Irish win. We got off to a bad start in this group six months ago and we needed to do something special out here to get back on track.'

The *Sunday Times* described Duff's display as 'a performance of consummate class'. Ireland skipper Kenny Cunningham was even more effusive when he spoke to reporters after the game. 'After the way he played in the World Cup finals in the Far East last summer, I'm sure there's not an international team manager who doesn't know about Damien,' he said.

'He is without doubt one of the best players Ireland has ever produced and now that his injury problems are a thing of the past he is going to be even more important than ever to our hopes.'

Duff's value to the Irish team was confirmed when, at the end of April, he was named ahead of Shay Given and Robbie Keane as the FAI's Player of the Year, twelve months after landing the Young Player of the Year title. 'This is a big honour,' Duff said, after receiving his award at a ceremony in Dublin's Citywest Hotel. 'I was happy with my own form but I wasn't the only one who did well. All of the other players deserve credit.'

In case anyone had forgotten why Duff had been crowned Ireland's best player, he served up another man-of-the-match performance in front of the Lansdowne Road crowd two days later, as Ireland marked Brian Kerr's first home match in charge with a friendly win against Norway.

Not only he did he score the game's only goal, finishing at the second attempt after his initial seventeenth-minute header was saved, but Duff again demonstrated his versatility by operating with some ease behind the front two of Robbie Keane and David Connolly – just as he had operated with some ease on the left and right wings and as a central striker in previous internationals.

'Damien is in such a rich vein of form for club and country,' Kerr said. 'He was very good, very good indeed. I thought the lads also coped well with the new formation and that could give us something extra, a different option.'

'Duff was a revelation,' added *The Times*, 'producing the same sniping runs that lit up the World Cup finals last year and that he has replicated for Blackburn Rovers this season.'

Ireland's win in Georgia, together with a 0–0 draw in Albania four days later, had stabilised their bid for a Euro 2004 finals spot. When they beat both teams in Dublin in June they were right back in the frame, especially since Russia had lost to both Georgia and Albania since opening their campaign with a 4–2 victory over Ireland that had signalled the beginning of the end for Mick McCarthy.

Duff played in the first of those successive victories in June, a 2–1 win against Albania, but missed the 2–0 defeat of Georgia due to injury. A scan revealed no obvious damage to the hamstring but there was inflammation at the back of the knee. It certainly wasn't the first injury scare Duff had encountered that season. His frequent battle against muscular niggles was a constant source of frustration, and he was prepared to try anything in order to rid himself of such problems.

That desire to register a clean bill of health led to a bizarre story that appeared in several newspapers shortly after those two Dublin internationals in June. 'Damien Duff inadvertently sparked a suicide alert after onlookers feared he was about to leap into the Irish Sea,' read a report in the *Express*.

It was, of course, a false alarm, but an amusing tale nonetheless. It turned out that Duff had been advised to soak himself in the sea because the salt water would have a healing affect on his aching limbs (it worked for horses, he was told), and he put the theory to the test before Ireland's clash with Georgia. One concerned member of the public was obviously unaware of such methods.

The *Express* article continued,

A distress call was made to the police after the 24-year-old was spotted in the sea at 7.30 a.m. by a worried passer-by just yards from the team's base in Dublin.

Duff emerged from the waves and headed back to his room, unaware of the panic he had caused. After combing the area for the mystery man, officers spoke to Irish manager Brian Kerr, to ask if any of his players were missing. It was then that the embarrassing mix-up was unravelled and a spokesman for Duff said: 'The whole emergency was a false alarm and the boys were laughing about it. The game was important but it didn't put Duff under that much pressure.'

Duff gave his account of the incident a few months later in an interview with one of his former Ireland teammates, the *Times* columnist Tony Cascarino.

'I had my hood on, and was listening to my Walkman so couldn't hear what people were saying,' he explained. 'I went back into my room and went to sleep. The next thing, I heard a big helicopter, boat and coastguards. Apparently someone who lives close to the hotel rang the police and said there is a young man trying to commit suicide on Portmarnock beach.'

Wading into the sea wasn't the first alternative method that Duff had adopted in his search for a successful remedy. Earlier that year, during one of the player's hamstring-injury-enforced lay-offs, the Blackburn physio Dave Fevre revealed that Rovers were exploring every possible cause of their greatest asset's ongoing problems. If their suspicions were correct, then to make sure he stayed out of the treatment room Duff would have to make big changes – to his car seat. Fevre reckoned that Duff's low-slung Mercedes could be to blame.

'A lot of players drive expensive cars and they can actually lead to problems,' he revealed to the press. 'The seats are lower, and you're often in a different position than in a normal car. In terms of posture, that can be nightmare. So we're looking at modifying his [Duff's] car seat. We've spent two days assessing everything, from his back to his skeleton to his bed. Then there's the footwear and how that suits your natural gait, so we've looked at many different things.'

The findings of the Blackburn medical team's extensive research saw Duff get a new bed as well as some inserts for his football boots. On the eve of his mid-March return to action against Arsenal at Ewood Park – almost two months after limping out of Rovers' League Cup semi-final clash with Manchester United – he spoke to the *Sun* about his injury nightmare.

'It's the most frustrating season I've ever had,' he said. 'I've been down in the dumps practically all season and I've never really got going.

'After the summer I was really looking forward to getting back into things. I started off the season well and felt brilliant. But then I started to get silly little injuries and then my hamstrings as well so it's been devastating, really.

'It does become psychological after a while. For the first couple of weeks back in training I still felt down and I was afraid to move in case it went again. But I've got my confidence up now, I'm nearly going at full pelt.'

The *Express*, meanwhile, revealed details of the alterations that Duff was hoping would bring his irritating history of aches and strains to an end.

'After three or four hamstring injuries in a season the club thought it was right to go through absolutely everything,' Duff said. 'They've even changed my bed. I've got one leg slightly longer than the other as well so I've got special inserts in my boots. They've also sorted my back out, because that was in tatters.

'I think we've sussed it now and I feel good so hopefully when I do get back, I'll be back to stay. I don't want to break down again. I want to be flying for the last eight or nine games.'

The results were astounding. Duff was on target as Rovers upset Arsène Wenger's Premiership leaders 2–0 and followed that by scoring in each of Blackburn's next three games as well.

By the time he'd claimed the fourth of those goals, to settle a home game with Charlton, some familiar old rumours had inevitably resurfaced. Duff had often spoken of his desire to play Champions League football and, although they were heading for a top-six finish, Blackburn couldn't offer him that. Those that could were eagerly standing by.

'It's vital he stays,' Graeme Souness told the press after the Charlton match. 'I certainly don't want to lose him and it would have to take a very, very special offer to make that happen.

'There's no doubt that if we'd had a fit Damien all season we'd have more points and we'd be higher up the table. He's a super player and he was the difference today. He's someone who runs with the ball and everyone likes dribblers, don't they? They get you excited, they get you on the edge of your seat.'

Watching at close quarters that day was Charlton substitute Jesper Blomqvist, the Swedish winger who won the Champions League with Manchester United in 1999.

'Duff was Blackburn's best player by a mile,' he said. 'The way he played was really impressive and he could definitely do well at United. It takes something extra to play at Old Trafford. It's more a question of being mentally strong to go and do well there. You can never say for sure but he's a class player.'

If Duff had finished the season in fairly unspectacular fashion then maybe the transfer talk would have gone away. But, on the contrary, Duff was showing no signs of letting up. Just as he had done in the previous campaign he saved his most scintillating form for the run-in. He scored six goals in Blackburn's final nine games to end the campaign with eleven in all competitions, and was Rovers' top scorer in the Premiership with nine.

During that spell, Duff also doubled his international tally with those goals against Georgia and Norway, so it was no wonder that Blackburn's assistant boss Tony Parkes admitted, 'If clubs are interested and pay the right money, there is every chance he will move.'

On the final day of the season, Blackburn recorded a resounding 4–0 victory away to Tottenham to secure sixth position and a place in the UEFA Cup. Three minutes into the second half of that match, the ball ran loose in the Tottenham penalty area and Damien Duff reacted the fastest to shoot past keeper Kasey Keller and give his team a comfortable 3–0 advantage. Rovers fans stood to acclaim their hero, unaware that the effort would prove to be a parting gift.

CHAPTER 12

Blue is the Colour

'We have the resources and ambition to achieve
even more given the huge potential of this great club.'
ROMAN ABRAMOVICH, JULY 2003

What is it that makes a team successful? Certainly a steely spine to the side, a smattering of 'match winners', a burning desire to be the best, the right blend of youth and experience, an inspirational captain and a canny manager. That'll do for starters. But what really helps, of course, is if the forty-ninth-richest person in the world takes control of the club.

That's exactly what happened to Chelsea in the summer of 2003. A thirty-six-year-old Russian billionaire by the name of Roman Abramovich, who sat just inside the top fifty on *Forbes* magazine's list of the richest people on the planet, strolled into London looking to buy a football club. A £150 million deal later he'd found one.

It was a move that shifted the balance of power in English football, and changed the life of Damien Duff.

Stories linking Duff with a move away from Blackburn were circulating long before Abramovich popped up in West London, of course. The beginning of that summer was no different, with his most likely destination still reported to be either Liverpool or Manchester United.

One club Duff wouldn't be joining was Celtic – not yet, anyway. According to the *Daily Record*, Duff still harboured ambitions of one day pulling on the green and white shirt of his boyhood favourites.

'I'd definitely like to play for Celtic but with the price on my head I think I'll be with Blackburn for a while yet,' Duff said. 'At this stage in my career I don't think it's the right move to make. In my opinion, the English Premiership is the best league in the world and if you want to improve as a player it wouldn't be the right move to go to Scotland.'

The noises coming from Ewood Park suggested that the money men were ready to cash in on a player who had been carefully nurtured at Rovers since arriving in Lancashire at the age of sixteen. Duff, meanwhile, had grown tired of the endless speculation.

'I am starting to get p****d off about it all, to be honest,' he told the *Sunday Mirror*, shortly after the Premiership season had finished.

'I signed a contract last year and now there is a ridiculous price on my head. I am not going to say what it is, I don't want to say what it is in the media, but it is a stupid price with the way the game has gone now. I don't think anyone will pay that sort of money for me even if I wanted to go.'

He also reiterated his desire to test himself on the biggest stage in club football. 'Everyone wants to play in the Champions League,' he said. 'It is the same for me, for Robbie [Keane], for all players in England. Just look at how much you can learn in that tournament. Josh [Manchester United's John O'Shea] has played 20 odd games or so in the Champions League now and it has improved him no end. The likes of Robbie and myself want to get there in the future.'

The press made a particular fuss over Duff's disillusionment with the 'ridiculous' offer – believed to be £17 million – necessary to trigger the release clause in his contract.

Duff was disappointed at the way his comments were reported. A few days after that initial interview, Duff was at the De La Salle school in Churchtown, where he was once a pupil, to help launch a new range of sports gear. It was there that he attempted to put the record straight.

'I made an innocent comment,' he explained to the *Mirror*. 'But I should know by now that it is going to get twisted and turned. When I said it I was probably p**d off with the speculation because I can't go anywhere without Liverpool and Man United being mentioned. We'll still probably be talking about this in five years' time.

'I am very happy at Blackburn and we will be playing in the UEFA Cup next year. Hopefully it will be a great experience. We also finished just two points behind Liverpool in sixth place and beat all the top teams, but didn't do well against those down at the bottom. So it is a case of "what if". The manager has done brilliantly with Blackburn, taking the club from tenth in Division One to sixth in the Premiership. Fair play to him.'

The arrival of Abramovich at Chelsea on 1 July changed

everything. 'We are delighted to agree this deal to acquire what is already one of the top clubs in Europe,' Abramovich said. 'We have the resources and ambition to achieve even more given the huge potential of this great club.'

Those 'resources' were seemingly unlimited. The new owner had accrued an estimated fortune of £3.42 billion through his various business interests – primarily in the oil industry – and he was eager to spend it on his new project. Chelsea fans couldn't believe their luck.

Within days of the takeover, practically every leading player in the world was tipped to join Roman's Revolution at Stamford Bridge. One of those players was Damien Duff. Liverpool and Manchester United had both spent the previous summer tracking him but neither was prepared to stump up the sort of cash that Blackburn was demanding for the player.

For Chelsea, however, money was clearly no object. For Blackburn, whose Premiership title success of 1994–5 had been funded by Jack Walker's millions, it was a familiar scenario.

Even so, Chelsea's initial attempts to land Duff were rejected because the amount of money they were offering fell below the escape-clause figure of £17 million that was stated in the Blackburn contract he had signed a year earlier.

'We've received two bids from Chelsea and we've rejected them,' Blackburn chief executive John Williams told Sky Sports News, ten days into Abramovich's Stamford Bridge reign.

'We don't want to lose Damien. We hope he stays. But there is a clause in his contract which we negotiated twelve months ago and if Chelsea meet the requirement of that clause, then it's out of our hands. Damien is then entitled to speak to any club who meets that requirement and it would then be his decision.'

With the financial clout that Chelsea now possessed it seemed only a matter of time before a sufficient offer would be accepted by Blackburn. Graeme Souness was resigned to such an outcome.

'I don't want to lose Damien,' he said. 'We always knew he was a very special player. We have no intention of selling him and we want to keep him here. But when Damien signed his new contract last summer he did so in the knowledge that someone could come in and offer a lot of money. We don't want to lose Damien under any circumstances – but we are realists.'

While the fight for his services continued, Duff was at Manchester Airport with the rest of the Blackburn squad as they prepared to board a flight to Washington on 16 July. The US tour was part of the club's pre-season preparations and Duff was still a Rovers player, if only just.

America was somewhere that Duff had long been interested in visiting having heard only good things about the country from his international teammates who had toured there with Ireland in previous summers. Unfortunately for him, he would have to wait a little longer before discovering the States at first hand.

Having checked his bags in and wandered through security, Duff was minutes away from boarding the plane when Graeme Souness pulled him to one side in the departure lounge. He told him that, after rejecting a third bid, Blackburn had finally accepted Chelsea's fourth offer for the twenty-four-year-old.

'Graeme Souness gave me an ultimatum,' Duff later told the *Irish Times*. '"Get on this plane or sort out this transfer." My bag was on the plane and everything. As far as I was concerned I was going to America, at last. Graeme Souness had been asking me every day that week. I was putting it off, shrugging my shoulders at him. I was just dying to go to America. I just wanted to see the States.'

So instead of soaring across the Atlantic Duff headed south for Chelsea, and talks with his prospective employers.

As Souness pointed out, the deal was far from done. Duff had long been linked with a move to Liverpool or Manchester United, so he'd had plenty of time to consider the implications of a short switch across Lancashire. But Chelsea, up to that point, had not been seen as genuine contenders in the race for his signature. Duff had some serious thinking to do.

Duff sought the advice of those closest to him, determined to take his time before making a decision. As the days passed and his future still hadn't been decided, the press began to speculate. Liverpool had signed Harry Kewell, so they were no longer in the hunt for a left-winger, but what about Manchester United? Duff, they proposed, was holding out for a move closer to home.

At first, it seemed a fairly feasible suggestion. The son of a big United fan, Duff had followed the club (as well as Celtic) as a kid and named George Best and Ryan Giggs among his heroes. The story then gathered pace when United missed out on their number-one summer transfer target, Ronaldinho. Duff's representative, Pat Devlin, moved quickly to dispel the rumours, however.

'At this point in time, there is only one decision to be made by Damien – whether to move to Chelsea or stay with Blackburn,' Devlin told the *Sun*. 'Blackburn have had an offer from only one club – Chelsea. There has been no offer or contact from anyone else and, at this stage, the likelihood is that it is not going to happen. It is silly for people to be saying Damien should go to Manchester United because that has not been presented to him as an option. Chelsea is the option on offer and we are forging on with that.'

United chief executive Peter Kenyon stamped out the possibility of a move to Old Trafford once and for all when he said, 'Let's kill the Damien Duff story straightaway. We are not in for him. There has been no approach to the club and no approach to the player, and there won't be. He is due to sign for Chelsea.'

On 21 July, that was exactly what Duff did. Following a £17 million switch, he became Chelsea's record signing, and replaced Robbie Keane as the most expensive Irish player ever. With Glen Johnson, Geremi and Wayne Bridge also on board, the 'Chelski' revolution was well under way, and more big-money arrivals would soon follow in the shape of Juan Sebastian Veron, Adrian Mutu, Hernan Crespo and Claude Makelele.

Before joining up with his new teammates in Malaysia to take part in the FA Premier League Asia Cup, Duff had a quick word with Chelsea TV.

'This was probably the biggest decision of my life and I

didn't want to rush it,' he said. 'It was just a matter of thinking everything through. I had seven great years at Blackburn and there was no big reason to move but in the end I decided a big new challenge was necessary.

'It looks as though great things are going to happen at Chelsea. It just feels right. It's a big, big chance and I can't wait. [The transfer record] is a great honour for myself and my family, but the most important thing is to do it on the pitch now and hopefully I can do it all for Chelsea. I can't wait to start.'

The following week the formalities were completed when Duff was officially unveiled as a Chelsea player at a press conference. There he gave his reasons for moving, and also gave heart to fans of his former club by suggesting that he may not have made his last appearance for Rovers.

'The lure of playing in the Champions League was definitely a big reason behind my decision to come here but so was challenging for the title,' he said. 'I've been training with my new teammates for a week or so now but already I've realised there are some world-class players here. I'm really looking forward to working with them and I hope they can help me improve as a player.

'The move came as big a shock to me as it did to Blackburn because it all happened so quickly. It took me about a week to decide as I rang everybody that I knew. I wasn't going to make a snap decision because it was the biggest decision of my life.

'I loved it at Blackburn and I'm very grateful to everyone at Rovers for making me the player and the person I am

Above: Robbie Keane, Richard Dunne and Duff enjoy the reception as the Irish team are cheered in Phoenix Park on their return from Japan-Korea 2002.

Below: Duff wheels away after scoring for Ireland against Russia in 2003. The lead was surrendered though, and Ireland's quest to secure a spot at Euro 2004 would eventually fail.

Recruited to Chelsea by Claudio Ranieri for a then-club record £17m in 2003 Duff continued to do what he did best – tearing defences apart. In his first season, despite injury setbacks, he scored six goals for Chelsea.

Above: Given a run in Europe, Duff celebrates scoring his first Champions League goal in Chelsea's 4-0 romp against Lazio in Rome, November 2003.

Below: Deceptively strong, Duff leaves Barcelona's Puyol and Albertini in his wake as Chelsea lose 2-1 in the Champions League, February 2005. Duff scored in the second leg, helping to take Chelsea through 5-4 on aggregate and into the quarter-finals.

Surging forward, looking for options, ball seemingly glued to his left boot – the classic
Duffer pose.

Above: Duff gets away from Patrick Vieira of France during the 2006 World Cup qualifier at Lansdowne Road in September 2005. Ireland again failed to qualify.

Below: Jose Mourinho, 'The Special One' and Damien's second boss at Stamford Bridge, was reluctant to let Duff leave Chelsea but recognised the Irishman's need to play more games.

Pastures new. Damien is introduced to the fanatical Toon Army, July 2006.

Duff picks up where he left off, this time in black and white stripes.

The Tyneside Connection. Duff and his fellow Irish Newcastle team-mates Stephen Carr, Alan O'Brien and Shay Given on their way to the UEFA cup qualifier against FK Ventspils of Latvia, August 2006. Duff's hunger for games, goals and glory could well be rewarded if he avoids further injury at his new home.

today. And you never know, in a few years' time I could be back as a Blackburn player again – please God.'

Duff's new boss, Claudio Ranieri, was delighted to have secured the services of a player who, he felt, could develop into one of the best players on the planet under his guidance. 'If he follows me, listens to what I say in every training session, then I think he will arrive at the top of the world,' said Ranieri.

'I have told him, "You are my first choice winger. We have too many matches for you to play every one, but if you are fit, you are in."

'He can play everywhere. He is my type of player. He understands the game and can see early what needs to happen. I have wanted to sign him for the last two years. I don't remember the first time I saw him but what sticks out is his speed and directness. I chose him because he is so clever and always tries to do something interesting. I like my players to be direct.'

As Duff said, one of the most appealing aspects of a move to Chelsea had been the opportunity to play in the Champions League; after responding favourably to the challenges posed by the biggest competition in international football, he was keen to test himself against the best that Europe had to offer.

He didn't have to wait long to satisfy that particular ambition, making his Chelsea debut in a Champions League third-qualifying-round, first-leg tie on 13 August 2003. The setting wasn't Madrid, Milan or Munich, but the quaint surroundings of the tiny Pod Dubnom stadium in northwest Slovakia, home to domestic champions MSK Zilina. The crowd numbered little more than six thousand.

It was not quite what Duff had had in mind when he'd dreamed of playing in European football's most prestigious event, but he revelled in the occasion nonetheless.

Duff was outstanding, demonstrating why Chelsea had spent more money on luring him to Stamford Bridge than any other player in the club's history with an attacking performance of the highest quality. He crossed for Eidur Gudjohnsen to score the first goal of the night – and the first of the Roman Abramovich era – before an own goal completed a satisfactory 2–0 victory for the visitors.

'Duff was the best,' said Ranieri after the game. 'Every ball he made was very dangerous'.

A decent start in Europe, then, and now Duff and co. could turn their attention to the domestic scene. In the preceding years Chelsea had enjoyed no shortage of success in knockout competitions, claiming the FA Cup, League Cup and European Cup Winners' Cup under the leadership of Ruud Gullit and then Gianluca Vialli.

Despite those triumphs, one major title continued to elude the club: the top-flight championship. Chelsea had consistently finished in the top six under Gullit, Vialli and Ranieri, but topping the table had proved beyond them as their wait for the league title fast approached fifty years. Surely now, with Roman's riches, they'd never have a better chance of ending that drought.

It was a challenge that Duff was looking forward to

tackling as he settled into life down south. The boy from Ballyboden was perfectly at ease in his new surroundings, relishing the chance of improving his game alongside Chelsea's glittering galaxy of world stars.

As the most expensive of Abramovich's new recruits, Duff had seen his profile raised, and with that came an increasing clamour for press interviews. Everyone wanted to know more about Chelsea's record acquisition.

Facing the media had never been one of his favourite pastimes, but Duff was happy to oblige on this occasion in an effort to introduce himself to his new following. He started off by revealing certain snippets in the *Evening Standard*.

'If you ask me to name the biggest influences in my career it has to be my parents,' he said. 'Yes, I sleep a lot,' he admitted, confirming his reputation as a champion dozer. 'But I read a bit, have the odd night out, a game of golf or snooker or what have you. I'm reading George Best's life story at the minute.' Luis Figo and Robert Pires were his favourite players in the modern game. 'They play in similar positions to me, do similar jobs and what have you. I like to study both and learn from them. That Pires is a class act, to be sure. Pace, goals, everything.'

When Chelsea had emerged as Duff's most likely destination that summer, some commentators wondered how he would cope with swapping the Lancashire countryside for the bustling capital.

'People seem to think that I'm some kind of country hick who spent all my time in the hills above Blackburn. That's just rubbish. I'm an Irishman and I enjoy a good night out and what have you – but only at the right time. I've come here to play football. Everything else can wait its turn, can't it now?'

And he was adamant that no amount of fame or money – the press estimated that his weekly wage was around £70,000 – would change him.

In another interview, this time with the *Mirror*, Duff spoke of the day-to-day life at his new club. Rubbing shoulders with players such as World Cup and Champions League winner Marcel Desailly would take some getting used to.

'I have to pinch myself,' he said. 'It is a bit like a dream. At heart I still am a big kid looking around at Desailly and others in the dressing-room. It's unbelievable – but I am really enjoying it.

'There's a lot of competition for places and some days that isn't nice when you're going in to see if you're in the team – or even in the squad. You don't know what will happen. It's totally different. At Blackburn you were expecting to play every week, here you don't know if you will even be involved.

'I suppose it keeps you on your toes and you can only improve. It's brilliant but it's frightening. Every day in training, there are twenty-three players who could be in the team – enough for two teams and one over. Training with them is frightening, but I'm loving every minute of it.'

Foreign players had featured heavily in the Premiership ever since its inception and, for some time, Chelsea's squad had been more cosmopolitan than most. Duff joined a playing staff drawn from Italy, Argentina, Cameroon, France,

Iceland, Denmark, Finland, Germany, Holland, Nigeria, Romania and Croatia. Surely there were all sorts of language problems. Not so, insisted the Irishman.

The *Sunday Times* delved a little further, quizzing Duff on several issues. He spoke kindly of Chelsea chief executive Trevor Birch, who had immediately made him feel welcome at the club, and revealed how proud he and his family were that someone should think highly enough of him to part with £17 million to acquire his services.

'This move just felt right,' he said, before suggesting that, although Blackburn had given fans the impression that selling him was the last thing they wanted to do, the directors readily accepted his substantial transfer fee. 'In the end it was the best thing for both parties. They wanted the money, I needed the challenge.'

Duff didn't have to look far to notice the difference between being a Chelsea player and being a Blackburn player. A quick glance around the dressing room or across the training ground was like taking a peek at a who's who of footballing superstars. That's what made the move so exciting for Duff. 'When we signed Veron and Crespo, I'm like "Whooaa!" To me, it's just a big buzz.'

It wasn't the first time that Duff had stepped into a star-studded environment. When he first joined up with the senior Ireland squad he found himself mixing with players he had spent much of his youth admiring on TV. He became overawed by that situation, so he was determined not to let the same thing happen at Chelsea. 'I've learned from that, and I've felt at home here,' he insisted.

Another topic of discussion was the management of his financial affairs. 'I get paid on the last Thursday of every month, from there my mam looks after it. I don't ask her what she does with it. I like to think she has a good head on her. I mean, she is my ma. If I need anything, I just go and take it out of the machine on the wall. That's how it works. I don't go around flashing the cash, that's not me. I came here for ridiculous money, I get paid ridiculous money. It's the job I'm in, it's not my fault. I didn't ask for the game to be like this. I play because I love the game. That, and the fact that it's the only thing I'm good at.'

By mid-October, Damien Duff could hardly have wished for a better opening to his Chelsea career. Seven matches into the Premiership season his new team were unbeaten, having won six and drawn the other, and the Blues' record purchase had opened his goal account in a 5–0 win away to Wolves.

His schedule wasn't occupied only by club commitments, though; far from it. His country was calling – and how it needed him to deliver. Brian Kerr had helped breath life into Ireland's ailing Euro 2004 qualifying campaign and, with one game to play, a finals place was still within his team's grasp. Kerr's men would have been in an even stronger position had they not conceded the lead Duff had given them in a crucial home clash with Russia five weeks earlier. That meeting ended in a 1–1 draw.

Standing in the way of Ireland and a summer trip to Portugal was Switzerland, the Group 10 leaders, on twelve points. Russia and Ireland were both a point behind

Switzerland, with a superior head-to-head record giving Russia the edge over Kerr's team in second place.

All three teams harboured serious hopes of progressing as they headed into the final round of games. As far as Ireland were concerned, the situation wasn't quite straightforward. First of all, they had to get *something* from their game. A win in Basel would guarantee them at least a place in the play-offs, and would see them qualify as group winners *if* Russia failed to beat Georgia at home. A draw for Ireland could take them into the play-offs, but only if Georgia were triumphant in Russia. A complicated scenario perhaps, but it was probably the best position Ireland could have hoped for after losing their opening two games of the qualifying phase.

Ultimately, though, there was too much ground to make up. As Ireland struggled to get going, Hakan Yakin scored to give Switzerland a dream start after just six minutes before Alexander Frei sealed a 2–0 win for the home side. Russia, 3–1 winners against Georgia, finished second in the group and Ireland were out. Sixteen months after creating so many joyful memories in Japan & South Korea, Ireland faced up to the fact that a major finals tournament would be taking place the following summer and they wouldn't be there.

A couple of months on from that sad night in Basel, Duff reflected on Ireland's tame exit in an interview with the *Irish Times*. The pain was still blatantly evident.

'We were s**t,' he said. 'We lacked even a bit of fight. No spark. No nothing. We were just c**p. I don't know why. Maybe we thought about it too much. We went out without a whimper. We disappointed all the people who travelled. We were a disgrace really. I don't know why. I can't figure it out. I came back to Chelsea and for two or three weeks I couldn't get into a gallop. Basel was the first time I've felt like a big player in the Irish team and I was disappointed.

'I've always loved working with Brian [Kerr], he's always got the best out of me. I love him to bits and love working with him and that was the worst of Basel. We didn't get Brian to a major tournament. He deserved better.'

Rome's Stadio Olimpico. A splendid arena, and exactly the sort of grand stage that Damien Duff had imagined gracing when he'd spoken longingly of playing Champions League football. Chelsea's visit to the Italian capital at the beginning of November 2003 gave him such an opportunity.

There they would face Lazio, in the fourth match of their Champions League Group G campaign. Having seen his team win two and lose one of their opening three games, Claudio Ranieri, returning to the city of his birth, was looking for Chelsea to consolidate their position with a positive result.

It turned out to be the happiest of homecomings for the boss. Ranieri's men were brilliant, recording a stunning 4–0 victory that their ecstatic manager rated as the most satisfying performance of his three-year Chelsea reign.

The pick of the goals was scored by Duff after seventy-five minutes with a skilful finish that capped a skilful evening's display. Dancing in from the left, he outmanoeuvred a couple of defenders before planting a low right-footed shot past Lazio keeper Matteo Sereni. Chelsea had a three-goal cushion and Duff had his first Champions League goal.

It wasn't the only time in the match that Duff was at the heart of a significant incident. Lazio defender Sinisa Mihajlovic, who should have been dismissed earlier on for spitting in the face of Adrian Mutu, belatedly received his marching orders shortly after half-time following two bookings – both for cynical fouls on the irrepressible Duff.

There was no way back for Lazio, and Chelsea had stated their Champions League intentions in devastating style.

'This result didn't come as a shock to us,' claimed Duff. 'We knew we were capable of winning here and that's what we came to do. The lads were brilliant. This speaks volumes for the team and for what a great squad we have.'

Not only were Chelsea progressing nicely in Europe, they were also mounting a serious title challenge. They lost just one of their first fifteen Premiership games (to Arsenal) and entered December in top spot, ahead of nearest rivals Arsenal and Manchester United.

A key player in that run was Damien Duff, whose move to Chelsea was working out extremely well for both him and his new employers. Although he'd sometimes been assigned the role of substitute as Ranieri lived up to his 'Tinkerman' tag, Duff had been in excellent form, creating numerous goalscoring chances for his colleagues and chipping in with the odd strike himself.

What's more, there'd been no evidence of the injuries that had so often blighted previous seasons. Unfortunately, a new setback was just around the corner.

On 20 December, Duff fell heavily during a Premiership match at Fulham's temporary Loftus Road home and dislocated his right shoulder. On his return to the dressing room, Chelsea club doctor Neil Frazer forced the bone back into place, but Duff was facing several weeks on the sidelines.

'When I did the shoulder, I could hear the big clunk and I knew,' Duff told the *Irish Times* soon after. 'It was sore. They took me in and gave me some morphine and put the joint back in place. It was more frightening than anything else, but there's instant relief once it gets popped back in.'

It was a massive blow to Duff, a massive blow to Chelsea – and a massive blow to Claudio Ranieri's mum. After the game the eccentric Ranieri revealed that his 'mama' was a huge fan of Chelsea's dashing wide boy. 'Damien is Damien,' he said. 'When I don't put him in the squad my mother, who's eighty-four, asks, "Why isn't Damien playing?" She kills me about it and that's true.'

The media lapped it up, and Mrs Ranieri's soft spot for the Irishman became something of a running joke. Duff's situation, on the other hand, was no laughing matter. It marked the beginning of a miserable spell for the in-form winger, who would start just four of Chelsea's remaining twenty-one Premiership games that season.

Duff was no stranger to injury-enforced breaks, and had grown used to dealing with the frustration that each one brought about. That's not to say he wasn't desperate to be tearing around the training pitch with the rest of his teammates, but he was able to assess the situation with a certain sense of perspective. 'Usually by now I'd be on my second or third hamstring injury,' he reasoned.

So Chelsea's crocked winger was in a relaxed frame of

mind when he reflected in the *Irish Times* on his opening few months as a Blues player. There had been changes to various aspects of his life both on and off the pitch, he explained. His fabled sleep-a-thons had been cut short for starters because he had to get up earlier for training – not to mention the fact that his mother had had a word. 'My ma was giving out to me for saying I slept so much,' he said.

The way that Duff was operating during games had also altered. As a Blackburn player he'd always felt as if the onus was on him to round off his dazzling approach work with a decisive finish. At Chelsea, the likes of Hasselbaink, Mutu, Crespo and Gudjohnsen could do that for him.

'I'm more confident. I never really had that at Blackburn. I've always come inside but I've played that ball [into one of the strikers] at least five times this season. I can't recall doing that before. At Blackburn I'd be head down and taking on as many as I could. I put the pressure on myself. All I want to do really is impress.'

The quality of Chelsea's playing squad certainly wasn't matched by the quality of the club's Harlington training ground. The outdated facility near Heathrow was incredibly modest for a club of Chelsea's riches, and a new complex in Surrey was under construction. Duff wasn't complaining, though.

'Here at Chelsea this training ground is a bit of a s**t-hole but I can't wait to get in every morning to train. It's never a job. I wake up every day and think I'm a lucky b*****d. I play football. I get paid so much to do it. It's brilliant.'

A darker consequence of becoming one of the game's most

talked-about players, Duff had found, was the increased media intrusion that came with it. That was something he could never get used to. An intensely private man, he has never been comfortable reading his own interviews in print, and on several occasions he has expressed his unease at dealing with the press.

'I just don't like speaking to the media,' he told the *Sunday Times*. 'I know some people crave it. That's not me. I don't like it. Journalists twist your words. I just don't like it. I want to play football. It's as simple as that.'

In an interview with the *Independent* he said, 'A lot of rubbish gets written. I've no real reason to talk to [reporters], I know it comes as part of the job but I'd rather just keep my head down and play football. I let the others do the talking.'

It wasn't that he didn't want to be in the papers at all: he just wanted to create headlines through his actions on the pitch, not off it. 'I never do interviews anyway,' he said in Ireland's *Sunday Independent*. 'I find it embarrassing, them articles. I don't mind being in the papers for scoring a goal or winning a match, but I'm not one for doing big, exclusive interviews. Most of us speak s**t anyway, they're a load of c**p. I just don't like seeing myself in the papers if it's not about football.'

On another occasion, he spoke to the *Sunday Independent* about an incident where he confronted a photographer who had snapped him and his girlfriend while they were strolling about Dublin. 'I chased after him and I'd do it again,' he said. 'They're the scum of the earth in my view. If it was me on my own I'd have no problem, that's what they want – but when my family and friends and my girlfriend are with me, I don't accept it.'

Life in the capital was, in general, treating him kindly, though. And he'd discovered a new pastime to rival his previous favourites of golf, snooker and, of course, snoozing.

'I love the musicals, the West End shows,' he announced. 'That's a thing I like about London. Brilliant.'

Mama Mia, 'the Rod Stewart one', *We Will Rock You*, *The Lion King* – he'd seen them all. The cinema was also frequented on a regular basis. 'I went to *Lord of the Rings* with me girlfriend and little brother at Christmas when they were over. Then the house was quiet again and there's a little cinema down the road, so I went, like a weirdo, on my own to see a love story.'

The move south may have changed Damien Duff's lifestyle but, it's safe to say, the bright lights of London certainly hadn't changed Damien Duff. An unshakably grounded young man, he nipped home to visit his family in Ireland whenever the chance arose.

'It's worth travelling a thousand miles for Sunday dinner with me mam, the family and girlfriend,' he said.

The injury-prone Duff had always embraced alternative methods of rehabilitation. At Blackburn, he'd had his car seat modified and his bed replaced in order to alleviate ongoing hamstring problems. He even tested the healing powers of the sea by wading into the ocean while on international duty to soak his weary limbs. If there was a chance it would get him back playing football a second more quickly, then Duff was interested in trying it.

So, when he was advised to engage in a bit of rough 'n'

tumble to aid his latest fight for fitness, he was on the mats like a shot. 'My shoulder's still weak, but I've been doing some judo to practise my rolls and falling on it,' he said on Chelsea TV.

'I've been trying everything really. I'm going to see another specialist now and I've been keeping on top of things. When I first went to the specialist, he wanted me to have an operation. But that would have put me out of action for three months, and I didn't want to do it because I would have been missing too much football. So I took a big risk by not getting it done, but I've been working hard with [fitness coach] Roberto Sassi. I'm hoping the shoulder will heal itself with a lot of rehabilitation work.'

That decision not to have an operation would come back to haunt him, although at first the shoulder injury didn't seem to have caused that much of a disruption.

Duff was back in action, as a substitute in an FA Cup tie against Watford, just three and a half weeks after suffering the dislocation. That, however, proved to be a false dawn. An Achilles tendon injury dumped him back on the sidelines as his New Year went from bad to worse. In the whole of January and February Duff saw less than eighty minutes of first-team action via three substitute appearances.

'It's been a nightmare,' he said in an interview with the *Sunday Independent*. 'Playing football is all I live for, especially being at a new club and being desperate to impress. Missing all those big games was terrible.'

Still, he wasn't about to bemoan his plight. He felt that he was a better player than the one Chelsea had fought so hard to acquire a few months earlier, and saw in his manager a devotion to the game that he himself shared.

'I think I've grown up. When I came here in the summer, I thought the price tag would have bothered me an awful lot but I just laughed about it, it doesn't bother me in the slightest. I suppose I've just got more experience and I'm more confident.

'[Claudio Ranieri] is football-mad. He works 24 hours a day for Chelsea. He's so passionate about the game and I'll get on with him... as long as he's playing me.'

What Duff was concerned with was the prospect that Chelsea's considerable squad might get even bigger. The arrival of Abramovich at Stamford Bridge and his subsequent spending spree had fired the whole club with excitement, but boasting the resources to buy anyone on the planet was not something that made the existing crop of Chelsea players entirely comfortable. No one was assured of a place in the side.

'I don't think the squad can afford to get any bigger,' Duff said. 'It's hard enough keeping everyone happy at the minute. You want to play every game, but you're not going to play every game. If more players do come in, some will have to go. I don't think I'd be one of the players to leave, I've only just got here, but you don't know what's going to happen at Chelsea. We've got so much money now we could buy anyone. You can't look beyond the next week at times. I want to be here for as long as possible. I love the club and the fans have been brilliant with me. I don't want to go anywhere.'

Duff's worst fears were confirmed when, on 2 March (his twenty-fifth birthday), it was officially announced that

Chelsea had agreed to spend £12 million on a new left-winger. The player, a twenty-year-old Dutch international named Arjen Robben, would be arriving at the Bridge from PSV Eindhoven that summer.

The press were interested in gauging Duff's reaction to the signing and they did so the following day. Significantly, Duff was at something approaching his lowest ebb when reporters caught up with him. He'd spent several weeks out of action. His team had just shelled out a considerable sum of money for a highly rated young player who would directly threaten his place in the side. He had spent the evening in the unremarkable surroundings of Aldershot's Recreation Ground, turning out for Chelsea's reserves in a 2–1 defeat to West Ham. And now he was being asked how he felt. The result was just the sort of response the newshounds were after.

'I must admit it was a bit of a kick in the teeth after two months out to hear about it,' he said of Robben's imminent arrival. 'It's been the worst two months of my life… I'll just have to carry on doing what I always do and work hard. Hopefully that will be OK for me.'

Robben did his best to play down the situation by reacting to Duff's comments in diplomatic style. 'Of course you're not going to be happy when the club sign someone to play in your position, but when you're playing at a top club it can happen,' Robben said in the *Evening Standard*.

'It shouldn't be a problem for Damien because we can both play in different positions. It's part of life as a top footballer and you have to deal with it. I'm confident that Damien and myself can play in the same team because we're both flexible.

I can play on the left or behind two strikers and I know that Ranieri sometimes puts the left-footed player on the right and the right-footed player on the left. I can play in all of the attacking positions, left, right and also in the centre, which is good for the team.'

While Duff's reaction to the Robben signing had been indifferent off the pitch, his response on it was positively outstanding. He marked his mid-March return to the first team with two goals in two wins, against Bolton (2–0) and Fulham (2–1), to help maintain Chelsea's title push. The new boy's arrival was still three months away but the Robben factor was already in effect.

Another incentive for Duff as he fought his way back to fitness was the scent of European glory that was wafting around Stamford Bridge. After squeezing past VfB Stuttgart in the first of the knockout rounds, Chelsea were into the Champions League quarter-finals. The big matches were coming thick and fast, and it was precisely why Duff had committed himself to Roman's Revolution.

'I like to think I've grown a bit since moving to London – and that's no disrespect to Blackburn where I learned so much,' he said in the *News of the World*. 'But the pressure at Chelsea is such that at times it seems like playing a different game. And I'm loving it.

'For me, going to the 2002 World Cup finals with Ireland is the biggest thing I've known in the game. But it's also a bit special to run out with your club team in the Champions League.

'Chelsea have given me that chance and it's simply been the

biggest bonus for me in moving south. It's given me a new insight into club football and hopefully there will be a spin-off at international level as well.'

The problem for Chelsea was the team standing in their way of a Champions League semi-final place, Arsenal. In fact, the problem for everyone was Arsenal.

As the final phase of the season approached Arsène Wenger's unstoppables still hadn't lost a single Premiership game. So even though Chelsea's league form was excellent – the Blues won seven out of eight Premiership matches in February and March – the freakish consistency of their London rivals meant they were mere outsiders in the race for the title.

'They're unbelievable,' Duff admitted. 'If it wasn't for them having such an unbelievable season, I think we'd be in first place. They're frightening.'

Arsenal's command over Chelsea was hardly a new phenomenon. By the time of their Champions League quarter-final second-leg clash at Highbury in early April, the Gunners' unbeaten run in meetings between the two clubs had stretched to seventeen games. Already in 2003–4 Arsenal had beaten Chelsea twice in the Premiership *and* knocked them out of the FA Cup. At least a 1–1 draw in the first instalment of their European confrontation at Stamford Bridge had stopped the rot for Ranieri's men.

With home advantage in the second leg Arsenal were still favourites to claim a place in the last four. The one player most likely to help Chelsea upset those odds was Damien Duff. At least that's what both managers seemed to think when they spoke on the eve of the titanic clash.

'[Duff] adds something offensively to their squad, without a doubt, and he's a major danger,' said Arsène Wenger. 'I feel he's had a great season. He can run at you with the ball, he can provide crosses, he can score goals. He is one we have to keep quiet.'

Ranieri had been criticised by those who felt that Duff was too often the victim of his manager's overtinkering, but the boss knew exactly what his record capture was capable of. His elderly mother was clearly not the only member of the Ranieri family to have been captivated by Chelsea's wing wonder.

'He is an amazing player,' said Ranieri. 'He has ability, speed, he can dribble, cross the ball – I want him to play as he can. Duff is the man who can open every door. He can score a goal and make one, too. His qualities are very important to us.'

A match preview in the *Independent* was equally effusive:

Whatever his deployment, Duff is clearly back to his best after the shoulder and Achilles injuries which stalled his season over December and January and left him feeling low.

The statistics are also revealing. The bald fact is that half of Chelsea's eight defeats have been inflicted when Duff was absent. Because he has made 35 appearances and not featured in 13 games, that is a noteworthy return.

With his unkempt hair, his unaffected airs, eyes that always seemed to need more sleep and his almost gauche ways, 'Duffer', as he is known, even by his parents, has been an unambiguous success.

So Duff was considered to be Chelsea's most potent weapon by almost everyone and, judging by the uncompromising manner in which they set about dealing with him at Highbury, that included the Arsenal backline.

The physical treatment didn't deter Duff, but it did help Arsenal reach the break without conceding. Even better for Wenger's side, José Antonio Reyes scored on the stroke of half-time to give the home team a crucial advantage.

But, although it may not have looked like it, Arsenal's rule over Chelsea was about to end. Frank Lampard drew the visitors level shortly after the interval, and then, with three minutes remaining, Wayne Bridge exchanged passes with Eidur Gudjohnsen before beating Jens Lehmann with a cool finish. The unlikely hero disappeared into a mass of frenzied away supporters at Highbury's Clock End, and Chelsea's Arsenal hoodoo had been well and truly busted.

For Claudio Ranieri it was the most satisfying of evenings. With Chelsea playing second fiddle to Arsenal in the title race, his future as the Blues' boss looked increasingly bleak. He was under immense pressure, and talk of Sven-Göran Eriksson – among others – replacing him at Stamford Bridge just wouldn't go away.

Ranieri's emotional response to his team's Highbury heroics was understandably defiant. 'It's difficult to kill me,' he declared. 'I may be "dead" but I will continue to work.'

Unfortunately for Ranieri, things didn't get much better

from there. Initially, Chelsea hoped that their success at Arsenal would knock the leaders sufficiently out of their stride to disrupt their unerring league form. The result could inject new life into the battle for Premiership supremacy, Chelsea reckoned.

But it wasn't to be. Arsenal responded to their Euro exit by beating Liverpool 4–2, and, with Chelsea drawing 0–0 at home to Middlesbrough, the gap separating the top two had been extended to six points. And Arsenal had a game in hand. Chelsea's long wait for the championship was not about to end.

Glory on the European stage also eluded them. None of the clubs that made up the last four in the Champions League – Chelsea, Monaco, Porto and Deportivo La Coruña – were considered to be among the continent's traditional elite. As a result, each fancied its chances of claiming the trophy, especially Chelsea.

Drawn against Monaco in the semi-finals, they were set for a decent 1–1 draw away from home in the first leg until a late capitulation – not to mention some questionable substitutions by the manager – saw the ten men of Monaco steal an unlikely 3–1 advantage.

That deficit had been cancelled out within forty-four minutes of the return match at Stamford Bridge, but another Monaco comeback secured the visitors a 2–2 draw and a 5–3 aggregate success.

It was seen as a golden opportunity missed by Chelsea, and Duff hadn't been able to contribute in either leg. A virus prevented him from taking part in the opening game, before disaster struck at the end of April. Duff had been warned by doctors that his decision not to have an operation when he dislocated his shoulder earlier in the season would leave him susceptible to a repeat of the initial injury, and so it proved. He suffered a second dislocation on the training ground and finally underwent surgery in May. His season was over.

On reflection, though, it was a decent campaign for Duff. He scored five times in the Premiership and once more in the Champions League, and carved out numerous goalscoring chances for those around him. Seventeen million pounds was looking like money well spent by Chelsea.

Roman Abramovich had plenty more cash to splash but, in the owner's eyes, Claudio Ranieri wasn't the right man to spend it. A runners-up spot in the Premiership and a place in the semi-finals of the Champions League wasn't enough to satisfy the big boss, and the likeable Ranieri was on his way.

Duff, who experienced a string of managerial changes during his time at Blackburn, had already played under a wide variety of managers at club and international level – Parkes, Hodgson, Kidd, Souness, Ranieri, McCarthy and Kerr all had their own inimitable way of approaching matters. The next one would be a bit different though. He was the Special One.

CHAPTER 13

Special Delivery

'He is better than I thought.'

JOSÉ MOURINHO, FEBRUARY 2005

'We have top players at Chelsea,' the club's newly appointed boss José Mourinho told a packed press conference upon his arrival at Stamford Bridge. 'And I'm sorry if I sound arrogant, but we have a top manager as well.'

As public introductions go, it was one of the more memorable. The 41-year-old Mourinho – or José Mário dos Santos Mourinho Félix, to give him his full name – turned up in West London at the beginning of June 2004 with a host of major titles on his CV and wanted everyone to know about it.

At Porto he had won five trophies in the previous two seasons, with his most significant successes coming on the European stage. In 2003 his team defeated Martin O'Neill's Celtic in a pulsating UEFA Cup final, and just one week before taking charge of Chelsea he'd guided Porto to an unlikely Champions League triumph.

That victory had made him the most talked-about manager in the game. The man himself was more than happy to join in. 'Please don't call me arrogant,' he said. 'What I am saying is true because I'm a European champion. I'm not one from the bottle, I'm a special one.'

Mourinho even had a word for his predecessor Claudio Ranieri, who had reportedly responded to rumours linking Mourinho with his job by suggesting that it was easy to be a successful manager in Portugal.

'If someone is Mr Ranieri's friend, could they contact him and tell him that I didn't win the UEFA Cup and the Champions League playing twenty Portuguese teams,' he quipped.

Mourinho's impact was startling. Not only was he refreshingly candid and outrageously self-confident, but the unconventional route by which he had reached the game's upper echelons made him all the more interesting.

The son of Félix Mourinho, who played in goal for Portugal and later coached in the Portuguese top-flight, José called a halt to an unremarkable playing career at a young age to concentrate instead on satisfying his coaching ambitions.

His first major break came when he worked as Bobby Robson's interpreter at Sporting Lisbon. Impressed by his knowledge and application, Robson made Mourinho his assistant and later took him to Porto and Barcelona. The experience provided Mourinho with a tremendous grounding, and, after going it alone at Benfica, Uniao de Leiria and Porto, he was now one of football's most respected coaches.

'I'm a great defender of team spirit and teamwork and the

first thing I have to promise to my new players is that I will look at them all exactly with the same eyes,' he announced.

So everyone at Stamford Bridge would be given a fair chance. Duff, though, wasn't able to make the best of first impressions on his new boss. Although he'd recovered physically from the shoulder operation that had brought his previous campaign to a premature end Duff was still wary of the injury. Having twice suffered a dislocation, he was finding it difficult – psychologically – to operate at his normal intensity.

'It's a hard operation to get back from, confidence wise,' Duff admitted to the *Sunday Independent* later in the season. 'I didn't miss any of pre-season, but I wasn't training 100 per cent or going into tackles and getting stuck in. I wasn't worried about impressing him [Mourinho], although it was at the back of my mind, I was just worried about my shoulder and getting back to being 100 per cent fit.'

After Chelsea's opening game, a 1–0 home win against Manchester United in which Duff didn't feature, Mourinho revealed his concerns about the winger's 'mental' state and suggested that a run-out in Ireland's friendly encounter with Bulgaria that week could help solve the problem.

'I tried to push Duff in our last pre-season games but he is not super-confident with his shoulder and he has to keep working on it,' Mourinho explained to the press. 'I don't think he's ready for Ireland but he is an important player for them and maybe this game will help him over the mental approach to playing in a competitive game again. I named him in my eighteen for the United game because I wanted to create a bit of doubt in the opposition's mind about how we were going to play. But he was never going to be ready for that game.'

Duff did play for Ireland in that match – a 1–1 draw at Lansdowne Road – but failed to start any of Chelsea's first seven games. It was an anxious time for the Irishman, especially as fellow left-winger Arjen Robben had now arrived at the club from PSV Eindhoven.

'It's not been the greatest of starts for me,' Duff told the *Independent* a couple of months into the season. 'I'm not starting games and have sometimes not even been in the squad. Maybe a couple of years ago, it would have got to me. It probably would have killed me off, to be honest. But I've stayed strong and worked hard. I'm not one for banging on the manager's door. I've just kept my head down and tried not to let it affect me.

'I'll take whatever role the gaffer wants me to play. When called upon, I will be there. We play a tight midfield at present with maybe someone pushing out on the left so there's definitely a place there. Maybe three or four years ago I was a bit more one-dimensional and would stand out on the wing all day. But I'd like to think I can come inside now and get the ball, pick passes, score goals and cause problems. I'll just have to push my way into the team.'

Duff had been aware of Mourinho ever since his Porto team had defeated Celtic in the previous year's UEFA Cup final.

'I saw then what he was all about,' he said. 'That he was a top manager and he wins things. It's been straight down to work with him. It's not about talking, it's about training.

240

There was a lot of chopping and changing [under Ranieri]. I don't think the new gaffer does anywhere near as much as Claudio did.'

If Duff was concerned about his future then he went the right way about allaying such fears. Once he was given a chance by Mourinho he provided the team with such an incisive edge that it was virtually impossible for the 'special one' to leave him out.

That chance came in a Premiership visit to Middlesbrough at the end of September, with Duff responding in some style. The chief tormentor in Chelsea's 1–0 win, he gave a performance that prompted Boro right-back Stuart Parnaby to announce, 'I'd say Duff is just about the most difficult out-and-out winger you can face in the League. He's that good.'

Parnaby's sentiments were clearly shared by Mourinho, as the Boro game marked the first of twenty-eight consecutive Premiership starts for Duff.

Mourinho's effect on Chelsea had been immediate. He began his Chelsea tenure by boldly labelling himself a top manager and his new team's impressive early-season form seemed to validate that claim. They took maximum points from their first four Champions League games and, on the domestic front, replaced Arsenal at the top of the Premiership in the first week of November.

Duff – making the most of his extended run in the team and adopting a more advanced position in Mourinho's system – was sensational, especially in the final stages of 2004. He started the following eight games within a five-week period leading up to Boxing Day, and scored in six of them:

20 Nov	Chelsea 2–2 Bolton	1 goal	Prem
27 Nov	Charlton 0–4 Chelsea	1 goal	Prem
30 Nov	Fulham 1–2 Chelsea	1 goal	Carling Cup
4 Dec	Chelsea 4–0 Newcastle		Prem
7 Dec	Porto 2–1 Chelsea	1 goal	Champions League
12 Dec	Arsenal 2–2 Chelsea		Prem
18 Dec	Chelsea 4–0 Norwich	1 goal	Prem
26 Dec	Chelsea 1–0 Aston Villa	1 goal	Prem

Significantly, all six strikes were the opening goals of each game. Duff had emerged as one of Mourinho's key performers, and the man in charge was full of praise for a player who just a few months earlier had been unsure of his future.

'I think he's playing fantastically,' Mourinho told the press after that Boxing Day victory over Villa. 'Duff and Robben, everybody thought only one could play and in this team they play together and it's not a problem for them and it's fantastic for the team. They can play left and right, inside and outside, they can shoot and cross. They have all these things in their pocket. They are doing that fantastically but also their defensive contribution is fantastic.

'I took Damien off because I know fifteen minutes for Damien means about two miles [of running]. If I can give him two miles' rest, it's important. I think Chelsea last season played four–four–two and he was a pure winger or left midfielder. Now Duff is an attacker with freedom and that freedom gives him a chance to play and a better chance to score.'

Chelsea began the New Year exactly as they had finished the previous one – in unstoppable fashion. They continued racking up the wins and, at one stage, kept ten consecutive clean sheets in the Premiership. By the time of their Carling Cup semi-final second-leg clash away to Manchester United at the end of January, Mourinho's men were ten points clear at the top of the table and still on course for a historic quadruple.

Having drawn the first leg 0–0 at Stamford Bridge those ambitions of landing four major trophies were severely tested at Old Trafford; by the end of the night, however, the dream was still alive.

Frank Lampard's goal gave the visitors a first-half advantage before Ryan Giggs levelled matters midway through the second period. Then, with just five minutes left, Chelsea were awarded a free kick high up in the United half just a couple of feet in from the right-hand touchline. Duff stepped up to take it and delivered an in-swinger that eluded everyone – most significantly of all, the United goalkeeper Tim Howard. The ball sailed over both attackers and defenders before bouncing into the goal just inside the far post, and José Mourinho could celebrate his forty-second birthday in style. His counterpart, Alex Ferguson, meanwhile, was left to contemplate the first domestic semi-final exit of his eighteen-year reign at Old Trafford.

With Chelsea challenging for honours on four fronts, Duff's busy club schedule was showing no signs of easing up. He did take time out, though, to celebrate a landmark in his international career on 9 February 2005. Almost seven years after facing the Czech Republic in his first ever senior outing for Ireland, he won his fiftieth cap in a friendly against Portugal.

Amassing a half-century of caps by the age of twenty-five is no mean feat, and in Duff's case it was a testament to not only his sublime ability but also his passionate desire to represent Ireland at every possible opportunity. While friendly internationals are considered nothing more than an unwanted distraction by some big clubs and their high-profile stars, the concept of passing up the chance to play for his country has always been alien to Duff.

In an interview with the *Independent* earlier that season he said, 'It's great being at a club like Chelsea, but playing for my country, especially at Lansdowne Road, there's no greater feeling. I just want to get as many caps as possible. I know in a lot of international teams you get people pulling out with niggling injuries, but I was devastated in the summer when I had to get my shoulder operation and missed four internationals.'

And, just in case anyone still had any doubts about his commitment to the Irish cause, Duff dispelled them by telling the *Express*, 'I will play international football until I drop. I love it and I treasure every Irish cap I have.'

Most of the pre-match chat centred on Duff. The man himself was reluctant to address the media on the eve of his special night, but at least Brian Kerr had plenty to say. And, predictably, it was all good.

'I think he's been immense,' Kerr said in a press conference. 'And for somebody so young to reach fifty caps still seems amazing when you think of someone like Chris Hughton getting fifty-three in an international career that lasted thirteen years.

'His performances in those games, though, have been fantastic. His work rate and honesty, the fact that he's always prepared to do whatever is required for the team – they're the things that are great about him and right now he's at the very top of his game.

The Irish *Independent* perhaps best summed up the impact Duff had made on Irish football, stating,

> It's only taken Duff seven years to reach a half century of appearances and in that time he has become the greatest player of his generation and easily the most exciting individual talent since Liam Brady starred in the green jersey.
>
> He may suffer from what Brian Kerr calls 'Adhesive Mattress Syndrome' such is his love of sleep but with the ball at his feet, Duff's dazzling array of silken skills have mesmerised opponents both on the club and international stage.

Rarely one to disappoint on the big occasion, Duff marked his milestone appearance by treating the 44,100 supporters inside Lansdowne Road to a typically inventive display. 'He was sensational,' Kerr told the press after Andy O'Brien's goal had given Ireland a 1–0 victory. 'Damien is certainly in the top world bracket at the moment.'

Although not everyone was willing to join the Duffer appreciation society – certainly not Portugal's Cristiano

Ronaldo, who engaged in an ongoing battle with his opposite winger and was the target of a cynical foul that earned Duff a booking – the plaudits were plentiful.

The *Daily Record*'s match report opened thus: 'Andy O'Brien's goal sank the Portuguese but it was Damien Duff's mesmeric show that really lifted the Lansdowne Road crowd. This may have been a friendly but the Chelsea winger again underlined his importance to Irish boss Brian Kerr as he ran the show on his 50th cap before being subbed to a standing ovation.'

After the match, Duff was whisked away from the ground and onto a private jet bound for London along with José Mourinho, who had been keeping a close eye on events at Lansdowne Road, and his Chelsea colleagues-turned-opponents for the evening, Paulo Ferreira and Tiago. The night's work was over for each of them, but the real hard graft was just about to begin.

Sunday, 20 February 2005, marked the beginning of an eight-day period that would have a massive bearing on José Mourinho's maiden campaign in his role of Chelsea boss. His men faced three testing road trips in that time: first up was an FA Cup fifth-round tie at Newcastle; then came the even tougher prospect of a Champions League clash with Barcelona in the Nou Camp; and, finally, the Blues were off to Cardiff to face Liverpool in the Carling Cup final.

The start of that series could hardly have gone any worse for Chelsea. Beaten by Patrick Kluivert's early header, the visitors finished the game with nine men following a serious injury to Wayne Bridge and the sending-off of goalkeeper Carlo Cudicini. Bridge couldn't be replaced because Mourinho had already made a triple substitution at half-time, but Chelsea's problems didn't end there.

William Gallas and Duff – one of the three players introduced after the break – picked up knocks that forced them to hobble through the final stages of the match and, as a result, both were rated as doubtful for the Barcelona game. Losing the chance of claiming an unprecedented quadruple as well as the services of – potentially – three key players was not the best way to prepare for a trip to the Nou Camp.

The meeting with Barcelona was a mouthwatering prospect for neutrals but one that both participants would rather have avoided at the first knockout stage. In the group phase, Chelsea had finished comfortably ahead of Porto, CSKA Moscow and Paris Saint-Germain in their section, while Barcelona had claimed the runners-up spot behind AC Milan in theirs.

The pressure was on, and the Chelsea boss went about dealing with it in his own inimitable way. There are many facets of José Mourinho's personality that have contributed to his outstanding success as a manager, and one of them was particularly evident during this intense period.

He adopted a ploy of diverting attention away from his players by taking the heat himself. It was an approach that had worked for him in the previous season when Porto faced Manchester United at the last-sixteen stage of the Champions League. Alex Ferguson had refused to shake hands with his opposite number after Porto's 2–1 victory in the first leg and accused the Portuguese side of behaving in an 'unacceptable' manner – i.e. diving – in his post-match press conference.

Mourinho was happy to respond ahead of the return in Manchester and jumped at the chance of stoking the feud, claiming that the criticism aimed at his team suggested United 'must be worried'. He knew that by engaging in such a public spat he would take the main focus away from his players and ease the pre-match pressure on them.

It helped his team progress on that occasion and he was hoping that a similar approach would benefit Chelsea one year on. This time he used the pre-match press conference to name his own starting XI – which later proved to be false – and, just for good measure, the predicted line-up of Frank Rijkaard's Barcelona as well. Naming their team, let alone the opposition's, a day before a Champions League game was not something that managers made a habit of, but, then, Mourinho had never been the most conventional of operators.

One name missing from his supposed line-up was that of Damien Duff. There'd been mixed reports coming from the Chelsea camp regarding the winger's fitness before Mourinho emphatically ruled him out of the contest. 'He cannot run,' said Mourinho. 'His injury is very painful, so he is out.' His injury couldn't have been that painful, though. Come matchday, when the official team list was handed in one hour before kick-off Duff's name was on it.

For someone who, according to his manager, 'cannot run' just twenty-four hours earlier Duff showed miraculous powers of recovery to instigate the opening goal of the game. Having beaten the offside trap and brilliantly controlled

Frank Lampard's pass, Duff raced away down the right wing before flicking the ball across goal with the outside of his left foot. Barca defender Juliano Belletti attempted to avert the danger but succeeded only in turning the ball beyond his own keeper Victor Valdes.

That vital away goal gave Chelsea a slight advantage at the break, but despite holding the upper hand Mourinho was an angry man by the time he eventually made it back into the dressing room. A member of the Chelsea staff had allegedly seen Frank Rijkaard speaking to referee Anders Frisk in the tunnel area, and after Mourinho confronted the Barcelona boss a mêlée had supposedly ensued.

Mourinho's fury intensified ten minutes after the interval when Frisk dismissed Didier Drogba, before goals from Maxi Lopez and Samuel Eto'o completed a miserable second half for the Premiership side and gave Barcelona a 2–1 lead to take into the second leg.

There was plenty more drama to come in the tie, both on and off the pitch, but in the meantime Chelsea had other matters to attend to. Losing to Newcastle and Barcelona had ended their hopes in one cup competition and jeopardised their chances in another, so it was with some determination that they approached the season's first domestic final in Cardiff's Millennium Stadium.

Its reputation may have been tarnished in recent seasons, but the Carling Cup still presented Chelsea with an opportunity to dispel quickly talk of a mini-crisis and hand their manager his first major silverware in England.

The occasion gave Duff the chance to add a second League

Cup winner's medal to his collection, three years after picking up his first in Blackburn's 2–1 victory over Tottenham. In those three years Duff felt that his game had improved significantly, due mainly to the Mourinho effect.

Speaking to the *Sunday Independent* before the clash with Liverpool, he said, 'I think working with Mourinho has helped me an awful lot. He's made me a lot tougher mentally and tactically and that's probably just from being around him. I think he's the best manager in the world, it may be high praise, but it's the truth. The gaffer's got so much arrogance, so much confidence that it rubs off on you.

The respect was mutual. '[Duff] is crucial to us, I cannot rest him,' Mourinho told the press before the game. 'He is better than I thought. Until you know a player, you don't know what is inside. When you work with him you see his stability, motivation and intelligence. He is very intelligent on the pitch.'

Just as their trips to St James' Park and the Nou Camp had been, the Carling Cup final was a highly eventful affair. Barely forty-five seconds had elapsed before John Arne Riise volleyed Liverpool into the lead and Rafa Benitez's side held that advantage until Steven Gerrard headed into his own net eleven minutes from the end. That goal took the game into extra time, when Chelsea's superior momentum helped them claim a 3–2 victory, thanks to goals from Didier Drogba and Mateja Kezman. Chelsea had a major trophy to put in the Stamford Bridge cabinet, and Duff, who played the whole 120 minutes, had his second League Cup winner's medal.

'Winning the League Cup wasn't one of our priorities at

the start of the season,' Duff admitted to reporters. 'It's the bread and butter of the Premiership that proves who's the best team. But it was important to get ourselves back on track. The standards we've set mean even two defeats on the bounce is a major disappointment – three would have been unacceptable.

'We're still grinding results out even if our football is not the prettiest. That speaks volumes for the squad. Everyone's built us up during the season; now they're trying to knock us down, but we seem to be doing OK so far. We have one trophy in the bag. We are also six points clear in the Premiership with a game in hand and confident of holding the advantage.'

Once again, Mourinho's controversial antics caused a stir. He reacted to Chelsea's equaliser by facing the Liverpool fans and raising a finger to his lips, although he later claimed that the gesture was directed at his critics among the media. Whoever it was aimed at, he was ushered away from the touchline and forced to watch the rest of the game on a TV monitor.

After a brief return to league action had seen Chelsea extend their lead at the top of the Premiership to eight points with a 3–1 win at Norwich, it was time to renew acquaintances with Frank Rijkaard and Barcelona.

Mourinho wasn't quite the perfect host, though. As well as accusing Anders Frisk of 'helping' Barcelona in the first leg (Frisk retired from refereeing later that month after receiving death threats, allegedly from Chelsea fans) Mourinho suggested in the pre-match press conference that Barcelona 'didn't need to dive so much'. That particular claim seemed somewhat cheeky, considering that the chief culprit of such histrionics, Deco, had honed his skills under Mourinho at Porto.

Unfortunately, many of football's most eagerly anticipated matches fail to live up to expectations. A clash between two titanic forces often sees both teams cancel each other out and the contest fails to justify its pre-match hype. This, however, was not one of those occasions.

In one of the most exhilarating starts ever witnessed at Stamford Bridge, Chelsea raced into a 3–0 lead within the first nineteen minutes. Eidur Gudjohnsen and Frank Lampard claimed the first two goals before Joe Cole split Barcelona's shell-shocked defence to allow Duff a clear run on goal. Without breaking stride, the Ballyboden flyer opted to shoot with his first touch, giving goalkeeper Victor Valdes little time to set himself. The ball zipped past Valdes and the delirious reaction of the home supporters could almost be heard in the Catalan capital whence the visitors had travelled.

That explosive opening put Chelsea 4–2 ahead on aggregate, but with so much time remaining a Barcelona response was inevitable. It did indeed materialise, and it was inspired by the best player in the world. Ronaldinho struck first from the penalty spot and then stabbed an exquisite effort beyond Petr Cech from just outside the area to give Barcelona an away-goals advantage at the break.

Rijkaard's men retained that advantage until fourteen minutes from the end, when John Terry rose to head Duff's corner past Valdes. Barcelona's protests that Valdes was impeded by Ricardo Carvalho were waved away, Chelsea held on to win 5–4 on aggregate and the majority of the 41,515 crowd inside Stamford Bridge celebrated unreservedly.

Chelsea's Champions League progress failed to disrupt their relentless pursuit of the Premiership. Between mid-December and the beginning of April the Blues won thirteen out of fourteen league games and drew the other. Duff was one of the first names on Mourinho's team sheet but, just as the season entered its business end, the Irishman's club campaign was curtailed by a hamstring injury.

He sustained the problem during a 3–1 win against Fulham that moved Chelsea to within striking distance of their first top-flight title for fifty years. One week later, on 30 April, he was absent from the team that won 2–0 at Bolton to clinch the crown. His contribution to the success had been immense, however, with six Premiership goals (plus four in the cups) and numerous assists to his name.

The loss of Duff didn't stop Chelsea from landing the coveted Premiership title, but he was sorely missed in Europe. Having started both legs of an entertaining Champions League quarter-final victory over Bayern Munich (6–5 on aggregate), Duff was forced to sit out the semi-final clash with Liverpool, a team with whom Chelsea had developed an intriguing domestic rivalry.

The significance of Duff's absence was not lost on Liverpool manager Rafa Benitez. After the first leg was drawn 0–0 at Stamford Bridge, Benitez told the press, 'Damien is a very good and important player for them. Of course, they have a lot of other talented players and different types of players whom they can use. Damien has been a key player for Chelsea and I am sure they were sorry he could not play. Maybe it was an advantage for us.'

On a highly charged night at Anfield, Luis García's early strike was controversially adjudged to have crossed the line and the newly crowned Premiership champions failed to find a way back. For the second year in succession, Chelsea had fallen at the semi-final stage of the Champions League, and for the second year in succession injury had forced Duff to play no part.

As well as missing the Champions League semi-final – again – Duff missed another important club engagement in May. This had nothing to do with his dodgy hamstrings, though. An estimated two hundred thousand Chelsea fans lined the streets of West London to pay homage to their title-winning heroes, but Duff was unable to join his teammates on the open-top bus parade. He'd missed a flight home from South Korea, where the club had played Suwon Bluewings in a friendly as part of a lucrative new sponsorship deal with Samsung.

'Apparently, there was a bit of a mishap with his passport,' Pat Devlin informed the *Sun*. 'He got it sorted out in the end, but by then it was too late to catch the same flight as the rest of the team. You can bet he'll be making up for lost time when he joins them all for more celebrations tonight.'

CHAPTER 14

Frustrating Finale

'I've been nowhere near my peak. I want to get it back.'
DAMIEN DUFF, FEBRUARY 2006

A lan Hansen was pulling no punches when he previewed the 2005–6 season in his *Daily Telegraph* column. 'If you become complacent, you are dead,' was the former Liverpool defender's frank advice to José Mourinho and his Premiership champions. Not that the Chelsea boss needed such a reminder. 'All the teams, they know that they have to improve a lot to take the championship from us, and we know that we also have to improve to keep the trophy with us,' Mourinho told the same newspaper. But how do you improve a side that won the title by twelve points, lost just one league game all season and kept twenty-five clean sheets in thirty-eight outings? With Roman's readies, anything was possible.

Mourinho opted to strengthen his squad by spending more than £50 million on Michael Essien, Shaun Wright-Phillips and Asier Del Horno, while he also welcomed Hernan Crespo back to the club following a loan season at AC Milan.

Despite this enhancement to the quality of an already exceptional pool of players, there were no guarantees that Chelsea would stroll to a second successive title triumph. There is an old adage that says winning the championship is tough but retaining it is even tougher, and the statistics certainly supported that theory. Only Manchester United had won consecutive titles in the Premiership era, and before them the great Liverpool team of the early 1980s were the last team to achieve the feat. Even Arsène Wenger's Arsenal – three times Premiership champions – had never managed successive triumphs.

Chelsea set about doing so in stunningly efficient fashion. They won their opening nine Premiership games, keeping clean sheets in the first six, and in the eighth of those encounters Mourinho's men became the first visiting team to score four goals in a league game at Anfield for thirty-six years when they dealt Liverpool a 4–1 hammering on the Reds' home patch. It was the first week in October and already the champions boasted a nine-point lead at the top of the Premiership.

Duff was among the scorers that day, sweeping the ball beyond Pepe Reina to make it 2–1 after Didier Drogba had deceived Sami Hyypia with a delightful trick. It was Duff's second strike of the season and, having retained a regular spot in Mourinho's favoured starting XI, the Irishman could rightfully reflect on a decent start to the campaign.

Although it seemed unlikely at the time, that afternoon at

Anfield represented a high point from which Duff's Chelsea career would gradually wane due to various factors. The first of those factors was an all too familiar foe – injury. This time he picked up a knock while on international duty. What's more, it came at the worst possible time for an Ireland team preparing to mount a final push for World Cup qualification.

Ireland's bid for a place at the finals had been boosted by the second coming of Roy Keane. With his old adversary Mick McCarthy off the scene, the Manchester United midfielder returned to the international fold for a friendly with Romania in May 2004, two years after leaving Ireland's World Cup party in a blaze of controversy.

Brian Kerr's decision to welcome Keane back into the team was not met with universal approval, but Duff, who'd admitted to wanting Keane back in the side, was delighted with the news. He had the utmost respect for his former skipper, and that was never more evident than when he spoke at University College, Dublin, in 2002 after being honoured for his World Cup achievements.

'Roy is the best Irish player I've played with by a garden mile,' he said. 'He's very passionate and I hugely admire him and he's great to talk to, even if it did take me four years before we had our first conversation!'

The battle for supremacy in Group 4 had been incredibly tight, with every single clash bar one between France, Switzerland, Israel and Ireland ending in a draw. Unfortunately for Brian Kerr's men, the only time that a meeting between two of the group's leading four sides didn't finish all square was when France visited Lansdowne Road in Ireland's penultimate home game. On that occasion, in September 2005, Thierry Henry's goal was enough to give France a vital victory and a significant advantage in the fight for qualification.

Defeat didn't see Ireland drop out of the reckoning, but it did leave them needing to win their final two games, away to Cyprus and then at home to Switzerland, to stand any chance of booking a place in Germany.

The first of those challenges was successfully negotiated – just about – with a 1–0 win in Cyprus, but that victory came at a cost. Just a week after starring in Chelsea's 4–1 bonanza at Liverpool, Duff was forced off with a knee injury and, following a scan, was ruled out of the crucial clash with Switzerland four days later.

Ireland needed to take maximum points to be sure of a play-off place, but without their talismanic winger, as well as the inspirational Roy Keane, who was also injured, Kerr's side lacked the necessary nous to unlock a well-drilled Swiss outfit. Two years – almost to the day – after ending Ireland's hopes of sneaking into the Euro 2004 finals, Switzerland once again dealt a fatal blow to Brian Kerr's dreams of taking his team to a major tournament. A 0–0 draw was enough to ensure the visitors a spot in the play-offs, as France secured automatic qualification with a comfortable home win against Cyprus.

'When you look at the top four teams in the group, there have been twelve games between Israel, France, ourselves and Switzerland. Eleven out of those twelve were drawn,' said Brian Kerr in his post-match address. 'The only match lost was our home game against France. The crucial goal was Thierry Henry's goal here. We've shown great desire and commitment but it was not good enough overall. It wasn't for want of trying. We have had a positive approach home and away and had a go but sometimes it has not been good enough.'

Apart from that obvious setback at home to France, Ireland were left to rue a couple of missed opportunities when they'd taken just a single point from games they seemed well set to win. They twice drew with Israel, for instance, after establishing an excellent position from which to win on each occasion. In Tel Aviv they held onto a 1–0 lead given to them by Clinton Morrison's fourth-minute strike for most of the match until they conceded an equaliser in the last minute. Then, at Lansdowne Road, they raced into a 2–0 lead inside the first eleven minutes but again allowed their opponents a share of the spoils.

Duff, denied the chance to repeat his World Cup heroics of 2002, was reduced to the role of despairing onlooker. By his own admission, he had failed to hit top form during the qualifying campaign and he had been helpless in the end to prevent Ireland's tame exit.

He later revealed the full extent of his disappointment in an interview that appeared in the *Irish Independent*. 'It wasn't a nice couple of weeks after the Switzerland game, trying to take it in,' he said. 'It wasn't a nice time. I know it'll probably only really sink in properly when [the World Cup] is on the TV this summer. But it hurt. It's all very well saying that I might have done this or I might have done that if I was playing. Words are cheap. It's doing it that counts. I know myself I had a disappointing qualifying tournament.'

What's more, his knee injury required minor surgery, so he couldn't even relieve his international frustrations by throwing himself back into domestic action. There were still exciting times ahead at club level, though, and missing out on the World Cup only made him more determined to fire Chelsea's European crusade.

'It's a huge disappointment for me knowing that I'm not going to the World Cup,' Duff admitted the following month in a press conference that preceded Chelsea's Champions League fixture away to Real Betis.

'But I'm looking forward to the rest of the season. The Champions League means I'm playing against some of the best players in the world and it has more prominence for me now because I'm not going to the World Cup.'

It was initially feared that Duff would miss up to six weeks, but he regained fitness ahead of schedule and declared himself available for the Betis game three and a half weeks after sustaining the knee injury.

'I'm fit enough to play,' said Duff. 'I've worked hard to get back for this game. It's a surprise because the surgeon said four to six weeks and it's three. But I'm a quick healer.'

The meeting with Betis was Chelsea's fourth game in ten days. They had beaten Blackburn 4–2 on the previous Saturday but before that they'd dropped their first Premiership points of the season by drawing at Everton and then went out of the Carling Cup to Charlton on penalties. It was a mark of Chelsea's standing that a run of one draw and then a penalty-shootout defeat had constituted talk of a crisis.

'Last week was disappointing,' added Duff, who regarded the Charlton defeat as a draw because the scores were level after 120 minutes. 'I think many people were seeing it as a crisis, or a mini-crisis, but we weren't. We didn't feel that way at all because it was only two draws. It shows how strong we are to bounce back in the way we did against Blackburn last Saturday. We were still positive. We had worst points during last season. The way we looked at it was that they were only two draws.'

Duff's rapid return to fitness earned him a tribute from his manager. 'Damien is a great player and a special character,' said Mourinho in the press conference. 'He is very important for us and a great example of how important it is to be a tough guy to recover from surgery like he did. The medical department is brilliant and worked incredibly well with him.'

A substitute appearance in Betis, in a 1–0 defeat, was followed by seven straight starts for Duff before injury struck again. His Achilles was the problem area this time, forcing him back on the sidelines in December.

As Christmas approached Mourinho and his finely tuned group of players took a step back from their busy playing schedule to concentrate their efforts on conquering new ground – the music industry. In a bizarre bid to top the charts as well as the Premiership, Chelsea released a CD, with the manager and each player selecting one song each for the compilation album.

The result was an odd mix of tunes involving artists that ranged from the Stone Roses (chosen by Ricardo Carvalho) and Spandau Ballet (Joe Cole) to Marvin Gaye (Robert Huth) and Jamiroquai (Hernan Crespo). John Terry plumped for 'So Amazing' by Luther Vandross, Lionel Richie's 'Stuck On You' was the choice of Frank Lampard and José Mourinho rocked it up with 'Run To You' by Bryan Adams.

The most idiosyncratic selection of all was made by Duff, who overlooked his favourite band U2 and instead chose 'Joxer Goes to Stuttgart' by Irish folk singer Christy Moore, a tribute to Ireland's 1988 European Championships victory over England.

It was all a bit of fun, of course, which is more than could be said for the chasing pack's pursuit of runaway leaders Chelsea. After falling to their first league defeat of the season away to Manchester United in early November, the champions reacted in a manner worthy of their title by taking maximum points from their next ten games.

Unfortunately for Duff, his personal fortune was not mirroring that of the team. In February, he was introduced from the bench during the closing stages of a 2–0 home win against Liverpool, only to be replaced himself five minutes later due to a muscle strain.

That kept him out of action for another couple of matches, forcing the frustrated wide man to adopt an increasingly familiar position on the sidelines. His ongoing battle for full fitness was beginning to take its toll, and, having had his season disrupted by a series of injuries, Duff was finding it difficult to establish any sort of rhythm. As he admitted to *The Times*, he was struggling to regain the sort of form that had wowed Chelsea supporters during his first two and a half years at the club.

'I've had a hard time since an Achilles injury in December,' he said. 'I know I haven't got back to my best.'

However well – or badly – his club career was progressing, Duff could always count on international football to provide a welcome distraction. At the beginning of March he travelled to Dublin for a friendly against Sweden that marked the beginning of another new era for Ireland.

His failure to lead the side to the World Cup finals in Germany had cost Brian Kerr his job, which meant that Duff was set to play under the third manager of his senior international career. As with the previous appointment, there was no need for detailed introductions when Duff met up with the new man in charge, because they were already very well acquainted.

After a series of seasoned characters, including Martin O'Neill, Alex Ferguson, Terry Venables, David O'Leary, George Burley and Claudio Ranieri, were linked with the vacancy, the man eventually named as Kerr's successor – Steve Staunton – had no managerial experience at all.

'Stan', as he is more commonly known within football circles, was the first player to win a hundred caps for Ireland and enjoyed a long, successful playing career with, most notably, Liverpool and Aston Villa. But his experience off the pitch was limited to a few months as Paul Merson's assistant at Walsall, so the Irish FA's decision to hand him the reins was deemed a massive gamble.

To add some much-needed know-how to the new-look setup, former England boss Bobby Robson was installed as a 'consultant'. The somewhat random pairing received a mixed reaction in Ireland, with some confusion surrounding the definition of Robson's role.

At the press conference unveiling Ireland's new management team, Staunton attempted to clear up such confusion. 'I'm the boss,' he said. 'I'm the gaffer. At the end of the day what I say goes, the buck stops with me. I will use Bobby in whatever role I see fit. He has a huge role to play, he's there for me all the time. He's done everything in the game. He's played at the highest level, coached at the highest level and managed at the highest level. If I can't learn something from this man, then I'm not the right man. His experience is going to be vital for me as regards the media – this is my first job outside of playing. And he's got more enthusiasm than some of the eighteen-year-olds I've trained with recently.

'To play for and captain your country is an honour and I was fortunate to do both – but to manage them is the ultimate honour. It is clearly the opportunity of a lifetime for me. I am fully aware of the responsibility placed on my shoulders by the footballing community and I understand the expectations that go with that. I know how much football means to the people of this country. We have the greatest fans in the world bar none – I have witnessed it. I was so lucky to have soldiered with them over the years. We have to get the team up and running again and give hope to the fans.'

The identity of the new men at the helm suggested that Duff would continue to play a major role in the Ireland side, just as he had done under the previous two incumbents. Staunton had witnessed Duff's devastating ability at first hand during their time as international teammates, while Robson had been keen on luring Duff to St James' Park when he was manager of Newcastle.

One of the first things that Staunton attempted to do was repair a relationship with the media that had become frayed over the years. His first act was to ignore the convention of sitting a couple of players behind a desk for a pre-match press conference and encourage several Ireland players to mingle among an informal gathering of reporters two days before the Sweden game.

A prominent figure in the group was Duff, whose international career had evolved to such an extent that he was now a senior representative of the 'new' Ireland. Almost eight years on from his senior debut, the proud Dubliner could now be labelled an 'old head', with his trusty sidekick Robbie Keane – now the captain – in an identical position.

While wishing Brian Kerr 'all the best' and admitting that news of his departure 'wasn't nice to hear', Duff was hopeful of a prosperous future for the Ireland team and was looking forward to helping Staunton's new recruits find their feet at senior level.

'It's exciting, really,' he told the press. 'I haven't had any time to take it all in yet but I'm looking forward to it. I'm close to Stan; I always got on great with him. He'll get us back qualifying for major tournaments, hopefully. That's all we care about. I just think there's a sense of excitement in the air.

'When I first came into the squad, me and Robbie were supposed to be the next big things. Obviously, Robbie did great and I struggled a wee bit and ended up not even in the squad for some games. So I know what it's like when you're a young lad coming into a squad. I'll help them in any way I can. I mean I love it here now, I love coming over, even for the friendlies. I never miss one.'

In a bid to revive the spirit that had helped Ireland achieve such success during Staunton's time as an international player, he brought a few old faces back into the setup. One of those was former 'sponge man' Mick Byrne.

'At ten o'clock this morning the first thing I saw was Mick Byrne on top of me, kissing me, while I'm still in bed,' smiled Duff. 'Not pleasant... Nah, he's brilliant. He's a special guy. The lads love him and his being here can only bring a good spirit back to the camp.'

Duff also discussed his own form, and was typically honest in his assessment. 'I've been nowhere near my peak,' he said. 'I want to get it back. Obviously I've had a couple of injuries in the last couple of months but I've been working hard to get back to 100 per cent fitness and sharpness. It's been a difficult couple of months, I've had to play through injuries but I'm back now pain-free. Obviously, I'm not back in the

[Chelsea] team but I've had an awful lot more lows in my career – at Blackburn under Brian Kidd and what have you. I've been there, done that. It doesn't matter. I still give 200 per cent every day, and that's what matters.'

The excitement that Duff had spoken of experiencing before the match was blatantly evident in his performance against the World Cup qualifiers Sweden. Showing flashes of brilliance and giving Swedish right-back Alexander Ostlund a torrid time, Duff gave a scintillating performance that was his best in an Ireland shirt for some time. The Ballyboden bomber was clearly enjoying life under the new regime.

Setting the perfect example to Ireland's younger breed, Duff claimed the first goal of Staunton's reign when he beat Ostlund and fired home right-footed via a deflection off Olof Mellberg. Further goals from skipper Robbie Keane and Liam Miller gave Ireland a 3–0 victory and the new boss a dream start, but it was Duff who stole the show just a day before his twenty-seventh birthday.

His strike ended a personal drought at international level that had stretched to almost twenty-eight months since his previous effort, in a 3–0 friendly win against Canada. After breaking away from a celebratory cluster of players, Duff made his way to the dugout and embraced his new boss.

'I can't remember the last time I played that well for Ireland,' Duff told the *Sun* afterwards. 'I actually thought there was a lot of pressure on us. There were 44,000 people at the game and I think it was a massive night for the likes of myself and Robbie because we had to deliver.

'It will be a massive blow not to be at the World Cup because that will be the second major championship in a row that we have missed out on. But I would like to think that I could still have a crack at another three or four major championships.'

Duff's virtuoso display against Sweden had not gone unnoticed by José Mourinho, who handed the winger his first Premiership start for six weeks on his return to domestic action. Chelsea won that game, 2–1 away to West Brom, and Duff kept his place in the starting line-up for the Blues' Champions League trip to Barcelona three days later.

Having been paired together at the first knockout stage for the second season in succession, the two contested a stormy affair at Stamford Bridge in the opening leg. Asier Del Horno was sent off for a late challenge on Lionel Messi, the ten men of Chelsea took a second-half lead and then Barcelona rallied late on to snatch a thrilling 2–1 victory.

Twelve months earlier, Chelsea had produced an astonishing second-leg performance to claim a quarter-finals place, but this time there were no comeback heroics. A 1–1 draw in the Nou Camp ended the Londoners' hopes of conquering Europe.

Mourinho responded by dropping Duff to the bench as the Irishman's brief revival was dashed.

On 9 April, an article appeared in Ireland's *Sunday Independent* stressing a concern over Duff's lack of match action – he rarely finished the games that he did start – and subsequent loss of form.

'Damien Duff rarely excites as he once did but he knows he is unlikely to get 90 minutes to show his form,' it read. 'He last played 90 minutes for Chelsea in December, and no longer plays for the club with the flair he continues to provide for Ireland.'

Duff remained on the very fringes of Mourinho's plans as the season reached its climax. For the FA Cup semi-final clash with Liverpool at Old Trafford Duff found himself flanked on the bench by fellow wingers Arjen Robben and Joe Cole, as Mourinho decided to start the match without a single natural wide man.

All three were eventually introduced but Chelsea lost 2–1 to scupper their plans of a double, and the manager was left to face a barrage of criticism. Mourinho attempted to defend his team selection after the game by suggesting that each of his wingers was underperforming.

He said, 'I don't know why Joe Cole has lost form, but it is a reality. We have at the same time Duff, with a lot of problems in his standard. Arjen Robben, when he was suspended for four weeks, dropped form when he got back into the team.'

After a wait of half a century for a league title, two came along in quick succession for Chelsea. But, although he picked up a second Premiership winner's medal after coming on as a substitute in a 3–0 title-clinching victory over nearest challengers Manchester United, Duff had not enjoyed the most rewarding of campaigns.

The bare statistics tell the story. In all competitions Chelsea played fifty-four games in the 2005–6 season. Duff appeared in forty of them but played the full ninety minutes in just six. He made twenty-seven starts and thirteen substitute appearances, and featured from the beginning of just eighteen Premiership matches. He scored three goals, with the last of those coming in a 3–0 win against Newcastle on 19 November.

'We have four quality wingers but one will leave this summer,' the *Sun* reported Mourinho to have said shortly after the season ended. Chelsea responded by stating on their official website that Mourinho had spoken to a Portuguese reporter and that his answer had been misinterpreted.

One winger would be on his way out of Stamford Bridge in the coming months, though. A wonderfully gifted performer who had played a major role in helping Chelsea end a fifty-year wait for domestic superiority. It was time to move on and weave his magic elsewhere. A new audience awaited the boy from Ballyboden.

CHAPTER 15

New Kid in Toon

'We've signed a player other teams wanted,
he's hot property and it is a major coup.'
GLENN ROEDER, JULY 2006

T he revolving door at Stamford Bridge that ushered in
high-profile signings Michael Ballack and Andriy
Shevchenko in the summer of 2006 was about to nudge
Damien Duff in the opposite direction. His departure from
Chelsea was virtually confirmed by José Mourinho when the
Chelsea boss spoke to reporters at the launch of the club's
new kit in July.

With rumours abounding that Duff was on the brink of
completing a short switch across London to join up with his
old pal Robbie Keane at Tottenham, Mourinho said, 'Damien
Duff is a player I like and I have a fantastic and open
relationship with him. Because of that great relationship we
are thinking together about all the possibilities. The
possibilities are he can stay with us or he can move to another
club. But he is a player we are happy to keep.

'In my squad there are always a few players I want to leave and a lot of players I'm desperate to keep. And there are always a couple of players I would like to keep but I have no courage to keep when I can't promise they will be playing 75 per cent of the matches.

'I like Damien as a player and as a person. I listened to him for a couple of hours and I could understand what he has in his mind. After that it becomes business. He's such a good player we will do good business with another club.'

When talk of a move to Tottenham cooled, speculation surrounding Duff's likely destination gathered pace. Inter Milan, Valencia, Blackburn, Everton and Liverpool were all reportedly interested, but the Irishman had his heart set on moving elsewhere.

On 22 July, Duff agreed to join Newcastle United on a five-year deal. Even though he had just a year remaining on his Chelsea contract, the transfer fee of £5 million seemed like an absolute steal for the Tyneside club.

Although leaving the Premiership champions was a wrench, Duff explained in his first press conference at Newcastle that the lure of playing regular football had been too good to resist.

'I'd not been happy inside for a while and I knew it was time to move on,' said Duff, who was looking forward to teaming up with his international colleagues and good mates Shay Given and Stephen Carr in the northeast.

'At Chelsea over the next four or five years you'll get players who are happy to pick up money and not play much. But it's a short career and all I want to do is play games – that's the most important thing to me.

'If it wasn't for me piping up I'd still be there doing pre-season, but I rang the chairman about three weeks ago and said if anyone came in I'd like to speak to them. I probably would have won more medals if I'd stayed, but I simply would not have played as many games as I would have liked. But I'm here for five years and I hope I can add to my medals here.

'I don't regret going to Chelsea, but I'm more excited signing for Newcastle than I was for them. Chelsea have the best squad in the world, with four of the best wingers around. The first two and a half years there, I played a lot, but in the last few months I had problems and didn't play a lot.

'I had a feeling – and the gaffer will back me up – that I wasn't guaranteed to play a lot. I took it on the chin and asked to leave. He has been brilliant with me and he understood the situation. But I don't think I've got a point to prove. I did the business down there, but the last few months were a bit of a struggle and this is a new chapter.'

Duff also explained the thinking behind his decision to turn down Chelsea's capital rivals Tottenham. 'I loved it in London and, yes, Spurs were in for me,' he said. 'But if I go to a club I put my heart and soul into it. For the last three years I've been a Chelsea fan and I couldn't go to Spurs – it's as simple as that. I couldn't sign for another London club. I spoke to people at Spurs and I told them that and I hope they understand.

'I had a great relationship with everyone at Chelsea.

Saying my goodbyes, I was an emotional wreck; I was in bits. I listened to my heart and it told me to come here. There might be some Liverpool supporters in Ireland saying I should have signed for them, but I just listened to my heart.'

Newcastle boss Glenn Roeder was delighted to have snared a player whose signing would go some way to easing the Newcastle supporters' dismay at losing Alan Shearer to retirement and then Michael Owen to injury.

Roeder was especially impressed by the attitude of his new acquisition. 'Damien's enthusiasm absolutely jumped down the phone when I first spoke to him,' Roeder told the assembled media at the same press conference.

'I really felt what he was saying was from his heart and truthful. He sounded excited about joining us. That's important in signing players, that you really believe they want to come, and that's the feeling I got with Damien.

'It's refreshing to have a top player prepared to come and play every single week, rather than just play some of the time and still pick up his cash at Chelsea when he's good enough to play there all the time.

'Unfortunately, with the squad that Mourinho's put together, that's happened to Damien, and it's happened to others as well, but he's stood up for what he believes in. Damien's every bit as good as the players he's left behind. It's fantastic in the modern game that someone has decided to come away from a team who are hot favourites to win the Premiership to help us win some silverware.

'If we can achieve that this year or next with his help, that will justify what he's done. We've signed a player other teams wanted, he's hot property and it is a major coup.'

Somewhat inevitably, on arriving at St James' Park, Duff was immediately likened to one of Newcastle's greatest left-wingers, Chris Waddle. It was a flattering comparison, but one that Duff was keen to play down.

'I don't need to be compared to greats like that,' he said. 'I want to be my own man and play my own game. Hopefully, I can become a hero like him, and I'm not saying I left Chelsea just to get worshipped. All I want to do is play football and be happy inside because I've not been happy for a while. I hope this is a place I can be happy.'

Glenn Roeder, who played alongside Waddle at Newcastle, also attempted to defuse talk that Duff was emulating the former England wide man. It hardly helped, then, when the man himself joined in the debate.

'We're different in some ways but I can see why people think there are similarities between us,' Waddle said in the *Sun*. 'Both of us look knackered after about two minutes and we'd not be described as perfect footballers. I think we've got similar running styles, though obviously I was far quicker than he is! Also both of us love to beat a man and don't mind dropping a shoulder and cutting on the inside. I like to think that, on our days, we could both be classed as entertainers.'

Duff made his competitive debut for Newcastle in a UEFA Cup second-qualifying-round first-leg tie away to FK Ventspils of Latvia on 10 August. Four days before that, Damien's younger brother Jamie had kicked off quite a week for the Duff family by making his debut for the Ireland under-18s against Malta at Dalymount Park.

The elder of the Duff siblings showed enough flashes of genius in his first few Newcastle outings to suggest that Chris Waddle had been right to label the Toon's new signing an 'entertainer'. After producing a delightfully deft flick in the build-up to Shola Ameobi's winning goal against Wigan in his first Premiership appearance for the Magpies, Duff then came up with a man-of-the-match performance in the return leg against FK Ventspils at St James' Park.

Twisting and turning in trademark fashion, Duff endeared himself to the home crowd by causing the Latvian defenders all sorts of problems and delivering a stream of teasing crosses that had Newcastle fans yearning for a predatory striker with the ability to take full advantage of such precise service.

All in all, the early signs were encouraging, and as far as Duff was concerned the future was very much black and white.

'I see myself finishing my career here at Newcastle,' he told the *People*. 'I'm 27 years old and I would like to think I have a good eight years in me. My contract here will take me to when I am 32, I will put my heart and soul into it and, hopefully, stay here after that. I am here for the long haul. Please God, we will win something. This club is massive – we have a great manager, a great board. It is all set up.'

Whether or not the club was on the brink of major success, one thing was for certain. With Damien Duff in their ranks Newcastle United's bid for honours was sure to be an exciting one.